Managing Children's
Disruptive Behaviour

Department of Social Policy and Social Work
University of Oxford
Barnett House
2 Wellington Square
Oxford OX1 2ER
England

Managing Children's Disruptive Behaviour

A Guide for Practitioners Working with Parents and Foster Parents

Martin Herbert
Emeritus Professor, Exeter University, UK

and

Jenny Wookey
Consultant Clinical Psychologist, Plymouth Child Development Centre, Plymouth, UK

John Wiley & Sons, Ltd

Copyright © 2004   John Wiley & Sons Ltd, The Atrium, Southern Gate, Chichester,
West Sussex PO19 8SQ, England

Telephone (+44) 1243 779777

Email (for orders and customer service enquiries): cs-books@wiley.co.uk
Visit our Home Page on www.wileyeurope.com or www.wiley.com

This publication is designed to provide accurate and authoritative information in regard to the subject matter
covered. It is sold on the understanding that the Publisher is not engaged in rendering professional services. If
professional advice or other expert assistance is required, the services of a competent professional should be
sought.

Other Wiley Editorial Offices

John Wiley & Sons Inc., 111 River Street, Hoboken, NJ 07030, USA

Jossey-Bass, 989 Market Street, San Francisco, CA 94103-1741, USA

Wiley-VCH Verlag GmbH, Boschstr. 12, D-69469 Weinheim, Germany

John Wiley & Sons Australia Ltd, 33 Park Road, Milton, Queensland 4064, Australia

John Wiley & Sons (Asia) Pte Ltd, 2 Clementi Loop #02-01, Jin Xing Distripark, Singapore 129809

John Wiley & Sons Canada Ltd, 22 Worcester Road, Etobicoke, Ontario, Canada M9W 1L1

Wiley also publishes its books in a variety of electronic formats. Some content that appears
in print may not be available in electronic books.

Library of Congress Cataloging-in-Publication Data

Herbert, Martin.
  Managing children's disruptive behaviour : a guide for practitioners
working with parents and foster parents / Martin Herbert and Jenny
Wookey.
      p. cm.
Includes bibliographical references and index.
  ISBN 0-470-84944-4 (alk. paper)–ISBN 0-470-84945-2 (pbk. : alk.
paper)
  1. Behaviour disorders in children–Treatment. I. Wookey, Jenny. II.
Title
RJ506.B44 H47 2004
618.92′8914 – dc22

                                          2003020687

British Library Cataloguing in Publication Data

A catalogue record for this book is available from the British Library

ISBN 0-470-84944-4 (hbk)
ISBN 0-470-84945-2 (pbk)

Typeset in 10/13pt Scala and Scala Sans by Laserwords Private Limited, Chennai, India
Printed and bound in Great Britain by Antony Rowe Ltd, Chippenham, Wiltshire
This book is printed on acid-free paper responsibly manufactured from sustainable forestry
in which at least two trees are planted for each one used for paper production.

For James and Rachel

About the authors

Martin Herbert is Emeritus Professor at Exeter University. He was previously Director of the School of Social Work and Professor of Psychology at the University of Leicester. He later joined the National Health Service full time and was in charge of the mental health service for children in Plymouth. This post was succeeded by a move to Exeter where he directed the doctoral course in clinical psychology as Professor of Clinical and Community Psychology. He was appointed to the Consultant Clinical Psychologist post in the Child and Adolescent Department at the Royal Devon and Exeter NHS Healthcare Trust. He now specialises in personal injury psycho-legal work. He has published books and journal articles on various topics dealing with the psychological problems of children, adolescents and adults. His latest is *Typical and Atypical Development: From Conception to Adolescence* (2003). Many of his books have been translated into European and Asian languages. He is a Fellow of the British Psychological Society.

Jenny Wookey is a consultant clinical psychologist at the Plymouth Hospitals NHS Trust and also honorary tutor and supervisor on the Clinical Doctoral Course at Exeter University. She has had many years of working with adults in GP surgeries and with parents and children at the Plymouth Child Development Centre. She previously worked in an adult mental health and primary care setting. Her special interests include developmental disability and young children with behaviour problems. In recent years she has worked with Professor Martin Herbert researching and conducting parent training programmes.

Preface

This book, with its four courses, is designed to help parents and professionals who look after or teach typical and atypical (special needs) children to gain, or regain, self-confidence in managing disruptive behaviour. It is organised so as to restore or enhance mutually enjoyable carer/parent–child interactions, and to reduce fraught interactions. The basic Child-Wise programme is made up of 'mix and match' (cross-referenced) components for use with groups of parents whose children (from ages 2 to 10 years) have behaviour management problems. There is also a home-based version for parents who prefer or need individualised training. The programmes are also designed to help foster parents and other surrogate (e.g. adoptive) parents. Attention has also been given to the use of the course by parents or carers with special needs children.

Because of the general importance of liaison between home and school when children display disruptive behaviour in both settings, we have included a chapter for teachers on behaviour management in the classroom. Joint home–school interventions have been shown in the research literature to be particularly successful.

Practitioners and would-be trainers from various healthcare and social services disciplines (psychologists, nurses, health visitors, and social workers), educational agencies (teachers, special needs teachers, and Portage workers), and child-care establishments (residential social workers and child-care personnel) have attended workshops on the use of the Child-Wise programmes.

A TV film, *The Trouble with Kids*, was made in 1999 in Bristol for HTV and Channel 4 television – a real-life, real-time portrait of parents of disruptive children attending the course over a period of several weeks. We occasionally use clips from this film to illustrate behavioural methods. However, it is a good idea to collect one's own video material from the widely available stock of commercial and TV channel programmes.

When practitioners have studied the text, and applied its guidelines in practice, they should be able to do the following:

1 Conduct a collaborative cognitive-behavioural parenting skills course.

2 Provide parents, other child-care personnel and teachers with strategies that can:

(a) add to their confidence as carers and teachers;

(b) increase their range of disciplinary methods;

(c) introduce them to problem-solving skills;

(d) reduce confrontational exchanges with their offspring or pupils;

(e) reduce reliance on inappropriate means of punishment;

(f) bring about improvements in the challenging behaviour of the child.

3 Help parents and surrogate parents to enjoy their caring, and allow teachers to enjoy their teaching.

4 Train others in child management skills.

5 Evaluate the outcome of an intervention using this programme.

Parents and teachers generally rely on common sense and intuition to work out solutions to problems for themselves and these are precisely the qualities we seek to draw out in the Child-Wise courses. We hope to promote positive parenting and teaching by an emphasis on constructive discipline, and by respecting participants' personal ideas and cultural values.

Because this is a workbook, the text remains fairly uncluttered with references. Instead, recommendations for further reading follow at the end of each chapter.

▶ How to use the book

Professionals from the mental health, social, educational, health visiting and child-care services can use the Child-Wise behaviour management programmes in groups or with individual parents who need support in coping with serious and 'not so serious' child management difficulties. The programmes are designed to help birth parents, foster parents, and other caregivers in their efforts to manage the challenging behaviour of children in their care. They seek to do this by developing carers' understanding of children, their development and the origins and meaning of their problematic behaviour. The programmes provide professionals with a framework in the form of a manual, for conveying that understanding to birth parents and foster parents.

In order to answer difficult questions and contribute credibly to discussions and collaborative problem-solving with participants, practitioners who work with the challenging and/or special needs children (aged 2 to 10 years) need to be well informed about parenting issues and about the maladaptive behaviours of young children, With this in mind, Chapters one to four of the book provide detailed background information relevant to the courses, and essential reading about their theoretical underpinning.

Material, in the form of handouts, assessment forms, rating scales and questionnaires, is available in the book for photocopying, with more proforma to be found on the Wiley website at www.wileyeurope.com/go/herbert. The various 'measures' do not provide definitive 'diagnostic' statements about the participants on the courses, or about their problems. They are not, strictly speaking, psychometric numerical scales. They are designed to help the participants avoid 'fuzzy' global judgements, by making finer assessments of children's behaviour and their own attitudes. They also serve as 'markers' that allow course leaders to monitor change in the parents and their children over periods of time, and indeed, their own performance in running the groups. The Child-Wise programme should not be considered primarily as a didactic training in behaviour management techniques. The social context of children's disruptive behaviours, their meaning for both themselves and their parents, and their impact on family and school life, should be part of the group leaders' remit.

PART I

Disruption by the child

Introduction

The Child-Wise behaviour management programme provides a theoretical and practical resource for parents and teachers who are struggling with children and pupils who are disruptive at home and in the classroom. There is growing concern about the anti-social pre-school and school-age behaviour of such children as it impacts upon carers, teachers and their peers. Their misdemeanours go beyond the day-to-day disciplinary problems familiar to most parents and teachers. They share an ingrained unwillingness or inability to conform to societal norms.

The term 'disruptive disorders' refers to a heterogeneous group of anti-social and aggressive problems, ranging from truancy and hooliganism to theft and vandalism. If children with *conduct disorders* (the extreme end of the disruptive behaviour continuum) are not dealt with at a young age, they are quite likely, as they grow up, to require multiple services from social, educational, health and judicial agencies. The increasing prevalence of childhood conduct problems has outstripped the availability of therapeutic resources to deal with them. Clearly, there is a need for standardised and validated courses for training parents and teachers of disruptive children of different ages – programmes that can be implemented by experienced and behaviourally trained child psychiatrists, clinical and educational psychologists, social workers, speech therapists and health visitors.

The Child-Wise programmes were designed with these goals in mind. They are rooted, at the strategic level, in *developmental and social learning theory*, and draw (at a tactical level), on *cognitive-behavioural therapy* techniques. The courses provide practitioners with methods that have an established record of enhancing birth and foster parents' confidence and skills when managing everyday disciplinary issues as well as the more serious challenges of emotionally and behaviourally disturbed children. Foster parents have frequently reported their desperate need for knowledge and skills to help them recognise and manage the behaviour of youngsters whose psychopathology or delinquency so often leads to the breakdown of fostering placements.

Attachment theory is an important theme in birth and foster parents' under-standing of the development (or failure) of parent–child emotional bonds, and if attachment is lacking, this produces insecurity, hostility, distrust and confused loyalties. The issue of 'bonding' is one that preoccupies foster parents as it has implications for their relationships with their foster children, their own children, and their personal feelings. It is also a subject of interest to teachers. All parents 'teach' and many teachers are parents; in both categories good relationships (bonds of respect and affection) with children are vital in order to 'fuel' and energise the learning process.

The Child-Wise manual contains four course variations of the standard version of the Child-Wise behaviour management programme. Chapters One to Three of the book serve as background material to the courses on disruption in (1) the child's own home; (2) the foster home; and (3) at school. Chapter Four is essential reading, as it details the critical theoretical underpinning of the programme. Practitioners will need to be knowledgeable about these issues in order to contribute to discussions and respond to questions with a sound knowledge base and in a style that is collaborative and creative. In other words, the Child-Wise programme should not be considered primarily as a didactic training in behaviour management techniques. The central aim of the course is to encourage, by means of Socratic discussion and respectful debate, parents' ability to solve for themselves the challenges their children present.

The programme includes the following:

- Well-tested practical courses to be used for treatment and training purposes. They can be used with groups of parents in clinical and community venues, with individual families in clinic or home settings, or in individual/group combinations. There are programmes designed specifically for foster parents.

- Materials for use by the client/patient during and after the intervention.

- Interviews, questionnaires, handouts and forms for assessment purposes, for evaluating course progress and outcomes, and as teaching aids.

- An approach to 'training' that is collaborative and therapeutic in the Rogerian humanistic sense.

- A basis for practitioners to assess *present* parental behaviour as well as a parent's *potential* for learning and change. These assessments have implications for children's welfare and related social services and legal requirements.

- Principles of behaviour management that enable parents, foster parents and teachers to translate their understanding of learning methods and child development into practical preventive and therapeutic tools.

- The promotion of 'positive parenting' by an emphasis on negotiated changes in carers' parenting behaviour and attitudes to their children.

Our hope is to instil or restore confidence in those carers who are confronted with demoralising 'difficult-to-manage' confrontations, by a partnership that respects their ideas, and provides them with empowering knowledge and skills.

CHAPTER ONE

Disruption in the home

Children in control – children out of control

The subtitle of this chapter was chosen to illustrate the plight of many hapless parents who feel that their children appear to *control* large areas of family life while being, in many ways, *out of control*. The title may seem hyperbolic when applied to defiant pre-school children at one end of the age scale, but not quite so exaggerated when we think of the highly visible anti-social and aggressive behaviour of some teenagers. In many years of practice the authors have met parents who feel bruised (literally and figuratively) and abused (physically and emotionally) by young offspring, as well as older adolescents. Others, we suspect, remain silent – too embarrassed to admit the intimidation that is part of their daily experience.

A mother attending one of our parenting skills groups shared her concerns about Coralie, her 8-year-old daughter.

Coralie displayed frequent temper tantrums and disobedience from an early age. Even before she was a toddler she wasn't easy, with her incessant restlessness and unending grizzling. She slept very little, which was exhausting. Although initially my partner Tom and I were told by the health visitor that she would grow out of these problems, we found that she became increasingly disobedient and aggressive. She was excluded from her nursery group before she started school. Tom and I tried every kind of discipline we could think of – threats, smacking, and taking away privileges. None of these worked. I'm convinced that her teachers blame us in private for her bad behaviour – saying that what she gets up to at school is unacceptable. They tell us that she has poor concentration and is hyperactive in the classroom. She bullies other children – particularly during breaks – and we get frequent phone calls to take her home from school because of what teachers call her 'uncontrollable behaviour'. There are threats of exclusion. Other children don't want to play with Coralie, and their parents are not at all friendly to me. Even my friends make it quite plain that although they welcome me to visit, it doesn't apply to my daughter. She's into everything and breaks things. It has all made me very depressed, and it has caused rows with Tom who says it's all my fault. He says I've spoiled her. If I've given in to her it is because she's so strong-willed that I don't seem to have any choice. Not that Tom helps much. I feel awful complaining like this because Coralie can show a very nice side to herself. The trouble is that it doesn't happen very often.

Troublesome children do not always display anti-social behaviour as extreme as that of Coralie. Their defiance and aggression decline in frequency and intensity at a slower rate and at a later stage of childhood than their peers. However, there is a hard core of children notable for their 'ingrained' unwillingness or inability to adhere to the codes of conduct prescribed by family, school, and the community at large. No less than 15 per cent of children can be described as 'oppositional and defiant' during the course of the first five years of life, the larger proportion of them coming from inner-city rather than rural areas. While about one-fifth of children move out of the high-risk group during the primary school years, others join it. Over half of the children and adolescents referred to mental health services are assessed as having disruptive behaviour disorders. We are primarily concerned in this book with these 'externalising' behaviour disorders – the diverse collection of disruptive problems referred to as 'oppositional defiant' and 'conduct' disorders.

▶ Definitions

In the fourth edition of the *Diagnostic Statistical Manual of Mental Disorders* (DSM-IV) (American Psychiatric Association, 1994), a widely used psychiatric classificatory system, Oppositional Defiant Disorder (ODD), is defined as a repetitive pattern of defiance and disobedience, and a negative and hostile attitude to authority figures of at least six months' duration. To meet the criteria, four of the following behaviours must be present:

- loss of temper;
- arguments with adults;
- defiance of, or non-compliance with, adult rules and requests;
- being a deliberate source of annoyance;
- blaming others for one's own mistakes;
- being touchy and easily annoyed by others;
- frequent anger and resentment;
- spite or vindictiveness.

These behaviours must be frequent and lead to impairments of social and academic functioning.

The conduct disorders (CDs) overlap somewhat with the oppositional defiant disorders (ODDs). According to DSM-IV, CD criteria entail the violation of others' basic rights, of age-appropriate norms and rules of society. At least three of the following 15 behaviours (categorised under four headings) must have been present over the preceding year to meet the criteria, with one present in the last six months:

1 *Aggressiveness to people and animals* (e.g. bullying, fighting, cruelty to people and animals, using a weapon, forced sexual activity, stealing with confrontation of the victim).

2 *Property destruction* (e.g. fire setting, other destruction of property).

3 *Deceptiveness or theft* (e.g. breaking and entering, lying for personal gain, stealing without confronting the victim).

4 *Serious rule violations* (staying out at night, truanting before the age of 13, or running away from home).

▶ Consequences of the conduct disorders

The consequences of children's conduct problems are serious enough in the short term. Victims are distressed by the anti-social activities of these children. Perpetrators also suffer a sense of failure as their anti-social behaviour becomes increasingly self-destructive. Repeated episodes of disruption in the home, classroom and playground – verbal and physical aggression towards parents, teachers and other children – lead to rejection by adults and children. It is not surprising, given that children with CD are exceptionally difficult to manage, that their deviant activities lead to exclusion from schools and sometimes what amounts to physical maltreatment from their parents.

As time goes on, the lives of aggressive, anti-social children are likely be blighted by severe problems. These include:

- interpersonal problems (e.g. dysfunctional partnerships and parenthood);
- truancy;
- alcoholism;
- drug abuse;
- risky sexual activity;
- delinquency;
- adult crime.

▶ Risks and protective processes: the early history

Estimates from prospective studies suggest that around 40 per cent of children with conduct disorders will exhibit anti-social personality disorder as adults.

Under-controlled (irritable, disruptive and impulsive) children at 3 years of age (according to a large-scale New Zealand longitudinal study, Woodward and Fergusson, 1999) were, in comparison with 'confident' children, at the age of 21:

■ twice as likely to have a diagnosis of anti-social personality disorder;

■ twice as likely to be repeat offenders;

■ twice as likely (boys not girls) to be diagnosed as 'alcohol dependent';

■ four times as likely to have been convicted of a violent offence;

■ much more likely to report having attempted suicide.

The family plays a major role in indoctrinating and training the child for life. In the early years, from birth to 7 or 8, compliance with certain parental requests and instructions is vital if the child is going to learn social, intellectual and physical skills. Among the reasons for enforcing particular rules are needs for:

■ safety – the child has to learn to avoid dangers;

■ harmony within the family – an aggressive, defiant 'brat' sets the scene for an unhappy home and disharmony between the parents and siblings;

■ the social life of the family – uncontrolled, destructive children are not welcome visitors and contribute to their own social isolation and that of their parents;

■ the child to have a repertoire of social skills and a maturing concentration span which will allow successful participation in the school's social and academic life;

■ the child to have an awareness of her/his responsibilities as a member of a wider community.

Parents and teachers use various techniques to teach, influence and change the children in their care. They give direct instructions, set an example, model desired actions and provide explanations of rules (i.e. use inductive methods of discipline). Behaviour is positively and negatively 'shaped' in the desired direction by using material and psychological rewards, praise and encouragement, giving or withholding approval, and other psychological punishments such as reproof or disapproval. At its simplest level this learning process is as follows:

Acceptable behaviour + Reinforcement = More acceptable behaviour

Acceptable behaviour + No reinforcement = Less acceptable behaviour

Unacceptable behaviour + Reinforcement = More unacceptable behaviour

Unacceptable behaviour + No reinforcement = Less unacceptable behaviour

When the family fails in providing appropriate and consistent socialising experiences, children seem to be particularly vulnerable to the development of anti-social conduct and delinquent disorders. Typically, children with persistent anti-social problems come from families where there is discord and quarrelling; where affection is lacking; where discipline is inconsistent, ineffective and either extremely severe or lax. It has been found that the parents of children assessed as anti-social differ from other parents. They tend to do the following:

- be more punitive, issuing more commands;
- provide more attention following deviant behaviour;
- be less likely to perceive deviant behaviour as deviant;
- be more involved in extended coercive hostile interchanges;
- give more vague commands;
- be less effective in stopping their children's deviant behaviour.

Data from the Oregon Youth Study (Patterson, 1982) suggest that the most severe behaviour problems start early, arising from a complex interplay between individual difference characteristics (e.g. impulsiveness, poor behaviour control, aversive temperament) and environmental influences (e.g. ineffective monitoring and discipline, dysfunctional parenting). A feature of families who produce children with conduct disorders is the prevalence of coercive interactions. The cues or messages are frequently negative ones, the 'sound and fury' of criticism, nagging, crying, shouting and hitting out being the norm. Communication between members may be impoverished or practically nonexistent. Parental ineffectiveness unwittingly reinforces their toddler's discovery that whining, temper outbursts, hitting and other aggressive tactics succeed in gaining attention. The likely outcome of family systems which control behaviour by the use of verbal and/or physical pain is children who exhibit frequent ('high rate') aggressive actions. Coercive interactions, maintained by negative reinforcement, are most likely to operate in closed social systems where the child must learn to cope with aversive stimuli such as incessant criticism.

▶ Developmental pathways and transmission of conduct disorders

There are two developmental pathways to the fully fledged CD condition: an early onset (before the age of 10) and a later onset during the adolescent years. The latter condition is difficult enough to deal with clinically, but is not usually as resistant to treatment as the early-starter version. Children whose conduct problems begin in their early years are three times more likely to develop violent anti-social careers than those youngsters whose misdemeanours have their onset at an older age. Children who display the more serious conduct disorders do not modify their behaviour as they get older. They retain conduct problems from the earlier years, simply adding more deviant behaviours to the previous repertoire.

Certain sub-groups of children with conduct disorders display more ingrained patterns of anti-social behaviour than others. Among the determinants (leaving aside the age of onset) are:

- the number of co-existing conduct problems (multiple types of conduct problems);
- the presence of Attention Deficit Hyperactivity Disorder (AD/HD);
- the possession of lower levels of intelligence;
- having a parent with an anti-social disorder.

There are three important aspects of co-morbidity to think about in planning treatment:

- the presence of AD/HD on top of CD leads to more severe and aggressive conduct problems, more persistent symptoms, and more peer rejection;
- the presence of anxiety in children with conduct problems seems to delineate a less severe disturbance, at least in pre-pubertal children. The moderating influence of anxiety may not hold, however, for adolescents with conduct disorders;
- the co-occurrence of depression does not seem to alter the course of conduct disorders.

Retrospective studies indicate that most anti-social adults have childhood histories of anti-social behaviour. And anti-social parents tend to have anti-social offspring. Having a convicted parent at the age of 10 is the best single predictor of anti-social personality at the age of 32. The mechanisms of imitation and modelling of, and identification with, delinquent parents undoubtedly play a role in this trans-generational pattern.

Costs to society

There are enormous costs involved in the apprehension and incarceration of offenders, and arising from the vandalism of public property. Of particular concern to the community is the feeling that much anti-social behaviour in young people has a mindless quality about it that defies comprehension. Reports in the media of parents being unable to manage their children, of anti-social behaviour towards fellow pupils (bullying, intimidation and blackmail), attacks on teachers, the flouting of the law on the streets (vandalism, muggings and hooliganism) all tend to confirm the public perception of life under siege. The most alarming aspect is that the incidence of crime, violence and wanton destruction increases as one descends the age scale. A small hard core of persistent offenders is responsible for a disproportionate amount of crime; the 1996 statistics indicated that 10- to 17-year-olds made up around 25 per cent of offenders convicted or cautioned for an indictable offence.

Prevention

A qualitative analysis of what parents said about their children's troublesome behaviour revealed a preoccupation with aggression, their dominant misbehaviour. They complained that:

- their children's aggression could take various forms and be directed towards different members of the family;

- they felt victimised; the children often acted aggressively towards them, to an extent amounting at times to a need to be 'on guard' in case the child should unexpectedly hit them;

- the children were unpredictable – at times highly tyrannical, destructive and defiant, and at other times loving – a rapid turnabout that caused particular distress;

- there were many incidents when their children had been destructive, causing damage to the house or household objects.

Can parents pre-empt the development of such anti-social attitudes and behaviour? Research indicates that 'authoritative' parents tend to raise children who have high self-esteem and who cope confidently with life. These parents tend to direct their children's activities in a rational manner determined by the issues involved in particular disciplinary situations. They encourage verbal give-and-take and share with the child the reasoning behind their policy. They value both the child's self-expression and his or her respect for authority, work and the like.

In the case of the mother (for example), she appreciates *both* independent self-will and disciplined conformity. Therefore, she exerts firm control at those points where she and her child diverge in viewpoint. But she does not hem the child in with restrictions. She recognises her own special rights as an adult, but also the child's individual interests and special ways. She uses reason as well as power to achieve her objectives. Her decisions are not based solely on the consensus of the group or the individual child's desires, nor does she regard herself as infallible or divinely inspired. This approach to parenting has been categorised as 'democratic'. Many persons other than parents have an influence on children's personality and behaviour but parents can encourage a strong 'immune system' in their offspring – protection against some of the stresses and snares of growing up. Such a system would depend, in part, upon:

- strong ties of affection and respect between themselves and their children;

- firm social and moral demands being made on their offspring;

- the consistent use of sanctions;

■ techniques of punishment that are psychological rather than physical, such as threats to withdraw approval;

■ an intensive use of reasoning and explanations;

■ responsibility given to children and adolescents.

These generalisations are guidelines that can be interpreted to meet the particular values and circumstances of clients. They are given in Appendix I, pp. 159–161.

Treatment

The central theoretical assumption of behavioural work is that much abnormal behaviour and thought (cognition) in children is on a continuum with normal (non-problematic) behaviour and thought. The laws of learning that apply to the acquisition and changing of normal functioning (e.g. socially approved) behaviour and attitudes are assumed to be relevant to the understanding and modification of dysfunctional actions and cognitions. Of course, there is much more to learning, and learning to behave in a deviant manner, than is conveyed by influences from the environment. The difficult task of restoring a reasonable balance of authority and control within the family is most effectively carried out, according to the evidence, by skills training for parents as individuals or within groups (variously called 'Behavioural Parent Training', 'Parent Management Training' and 'Behaviour Management Training') (see p. 43). Manuals describing behaviour management training can meet, in part, the need for widely available, standardised and economical interventions, referred to earlier. This approach directly addresses major conditions (e.g. failures of parenting and socialisation) that are known to contribute causally to childhood behaviour problems.

The therapeutic methods derive (at the strategic level) from *Social Learning Theory* and (at the tactical level) from *Cognitive-Behavioural Therapy*. *Behavioural Parent Training* (BPT) refers to programmes that train parents to manage their child's behavioural problems in the home and at school. In BPT parent–child interactions are modified by social learning principles and techniques in ways that are designed to promote pro-social child behaviour and to reduce anti-social or oppositional defiant behaviour. Procedures and typical 'scenarios' are practised in the individual or group sessions and then applied at home. Both types are discussed in later chapters. Extensive studies indicate the remarkable success of this approach in dealing with disruptive behaviour disorders.

▶ Select bibliography

American Psychiatric Association (1994) *Diagnostic Statistical Manual of Mental Disorders IV*. Washington, DC: American Psychiatric Association.

Bank, L., Patterson, G. and Reid, J.B. (1989) Delinquency prevention through training parents in family management. *Behavior Analyst*, 3, 75–82.

Brestan, E.V. and Eyberg, S.M. (1998) Effective psychosocial treatment of conduct-disordered children and adolescents: 29 years, 82 studies, 5275 children. *Journal of Clinical Child Psychology*, 27, 180–189.

Farrington, D. (1995) The Twelfth Jack Tizard Memorial Lecture: The development of offending behaviour from childhood. *Journal of Child Psychology and Psychiatry*, 36, 929–964.

Herbert, M. (1998) *Conduct Disorders of Childhood and Adolescence*, 2nd edn. Chichester: Wiley.

Herbert, M. (2003) *Typical and Atypical Development: From Conception to Adolescence*. Oxford: BPS Blackwell.

Kazdin, A.E. (1998) Psychosocial treatments for conduct disorder in children. In P. Nathan and J. Gorman (eds) *A Guide to Treatments That Work*. New York: Oxford University Press.

Lahey, B.B., Waldman, I.D. and Burnett, K. (1999) The development of antisocial behaviours: an integrative causal model. *Journal of Child Psychology and Psychiatry*, 40, 669–682.

Loeber, R. and Hay, D.F. (1997) Key issues in the development of aggression and violence from childhood to early adulthood. *Annual Review of Psychology*, 48, 371–410.

Loeber, R., Green, S.M., Lahey, B.B. et al. (1992) Developmental sequences in the age of onset of disruptive child behaviours. *Journal of Child and Family Studies*, 1, 21–41.

Meltzer, H., Garwood, R. et al. (2000) *The Mental Health of Children and Adolescents in Great Britain*. London: Office of National Statistics.

Patterson, G. (1982) *Coercive Family Process*. Eugene, OR: Castalia.

Rutter, M. and Taylor, E. (2002) Clinical assessment and diagnostic formulation. In M. Rutter and E. Taylor (eds) *Child and Adolescent Psychiatry*. Oxford: Blackwell Science.

Scott, S. (2002) Parent training programmes. In M. Rutter and E. Taylor (eds) *Child and Adolescent Psychiatry*. Oxford: Blackwell Science.

Serketich, W. and Dumas, J. (1996) The effectiveness of behavioural parent training to modify antisocial behaviour in children. *Behavior Therapy*, 27, 171–186.

Taylor, T.K. and Biglan, A. (1998) Behavioural family interventions for improving child-rearing: a review of the literature for clinicians and policy makers. *Clinical Child and Family Psychology Review*, 1, 41–60.

Webster-Stratton, C. and Herbert, M. (1994) *Troubled Families: Problem Children. Working with Parents: A Collaborative Process*. Chichester: Wiley.

Woodward, L.J. and Fergusson, D.M. (1999) Childhood peer relationship problems and psychosocial adjustment in late adolescence. *Journal of Abnormal Child Psychology*, 27, 87–104.

CHAPTER TWO

Disruption in the foster home

There are times when, for a variety of reasons, children cannot remain with their birth families and alternative arrangements have to be made. Countries like the UK and the USA, which are committed to the nuclear family, prefer to place the children for adoption or fostering. Some 65 per cent are 'looked after' (to use the contemporary terminology) in foster homes in England and Wales, more in the case of children under 10 years of age; 6 per cent are placed for adoption. The study of parenting behaviour in such families is not only of interest in itself but also helps to illuminate features of normal parent–child relationships which tend to be taken for granted.

▶ Fostering

The 'typical' home background

Caution is required when using the term 'normal' about family life. Our ideas in the West about the 'typical household' have changed dramatically in a relatively short time. For example, in the early 1960s some 90 per cent of children and teenagers were raised in homes with two married birth parents; today the figures are around 59 per cent in the UK and 40 per cent in the USA. This marked reduction in numbers is due to the dramatic increase in divorces and separations. The statistics indicate that an increasing number of children spend periods of their childhood and teenage years in homes with divorced, remarried, single parents, step-parents and with step- or half-siblings. Reconstituted families, in which one or both partners are combining two families into one, are another common phenomenon. The difficulties of being a step-child or step-parent are legendary. Some of the difficulties – the several adjustments to a new family with its various members in their 'established' positions – are similar for children in care.

Many have to deal with multiple 'transitions'. Transitions include transferring from family of origin to a foster home (and periodically back again), from placement to placement, moving into short-term care, moving from short-term to long-term foster care, moving into permanence through adoptions and eventually, leaving care. Throughout these transitions, children also have, if possible, to maintain links with their families of origin to whom they frequently gravitate as young adults.

'Looked-after children'

The term 'looked-after children' was introduced following the implementation of the Children Act, 1989, and denotes all children in the care of local authorities in England and Wales. It suggests a temporary provisional state and stresses continuing parental responsibility, even when the parents are not physically caring for their children. 'Looked-after' replaces the previous phrase 'in the care of'. There are two main categories of looked-after (foster) children:

1 *In care* – children who are subject to Court orders (e.g. owing to neglect, abuse, or being beyond control); on emergency protection orders; or remanded by the Courts pending further hearings.

2 *Accommodated* – children coming into care for more than 24 hours under Section 20 of the Act, by voluntary agreement of parents or guardians.

Nearly 50 children in every 10,000 are looked after by local authorities in England and Wales; the figure is 75 in every 10,000 in the USA. The number of children looked after for more than six months (70,000) has increased significantly since 1994 according to the Department of Health (1998). The vast majority of looked-after children come from multiply deprived backgrounds. Others are fostered because of parental health problems, the parents' need for respite, child maltreatment and neglect. The Children Act requires careful planning of admissions into care with parents and children. In practice, this often fails to happen.

Care plans

The circumstances of fostering depend on the following:

- the aims and objectives of care plans;
- the time-span (short term vs long term) involved;
- specialist (e.g. treatment-orientated) care;
- extended family fostering (kinship foster care);
- the make-up (e.g. membership) of the fostering family, and so on.

There is a preference, following John Bowlby's (1969) seminal research on the adverse effects of premature separation of an infant from the mother or mother-substitute, to maintain a child in the family home. If this is not feasible, a hierarchy of choices of out-of-home placements comes into play, favouring adoption first, then fostering, and lastly residential care.

Foster children are notoriously moved about 'from pillar to post'. The child may be fully aware (indeed, should be informed if old enough) that yet another change in his or her life is being planned. It happens quite frequently that children spend brief periods in foster or residential care interspersed with periods in what are often less than favourable own-home environments. Some children are likely to return eventually to their families of origin; for others this opportunity (if such it is) may be not very likely or it may be non-existent. Children may get regular visits from birth parents, have irregular contacts (with many broken promises), or get none at all. Hope is eternal for some children; others despair, become cynical, and eventually lose all trust in adults.

Which relationships are most important for looked-after children? In the case of children in residential care:

- over 50 per cent wanted more contact with siblings;

- one-third wished for more contact (25 per cent less) with mothers;

- a significant number wished for more contact with former foster carers.

Foster care differs markedly from residential care for the following reasons:

- New attachments are more possible in foster care.

- The carers in foster homes are older and maintain better emotional and sexual boundaries.

- They establish more effective limits on children's and adolescents' behaviour.

- Their management (e.g. verbal) strategies are warmer, more appropriate, more informative and more effective than residential carers.

- Placements in foster homes are more child-orientated and have better physical amenities.

- They provide more community contacts.

Looked-after children tend to love their birth families and think they are loved in turn. This poignant paradox exists despite the fact that they are in care because (more often than not) they were maltreated in their homes. One year into their placements they still think and dream about their birth parents. Nevertheless, they tend to rate their emotional involvement with both their birth parents and carers as low. Studies depict these children as yearning in vain for closeness and support. The reciprocity of trusting is not easy to find in their lives.

Consequences of being in care

The placement of healthy babies in *adoptive homes* appears to occur with no more long-term adverse effects than for children who never experience separation from their birth families. But what of children who have a history of abuse, neglect, abandonment and other tragic events in their lives? Adverse outcomes in mental health, education and social adjustment are characteristic of looked-after children as compared with other children. They have high rates of behavioural, emotional and mental health problems, and tend to suffer from significant cognitive deficits. Between 29 and 39 per cent of long-term foster care children (ages 5 to 15), when tested on the Rutter A Scale, were at, or above, the 'disturbance' threshold. About the same proportion of boys and girls achieved test results beyond the cut-off point on a scale measuring psychopathology.

Insecure attachments commonly result from the frequent separations from, and abandonments by, loved ones. Such insecurity predisposes sufferers to social and other problems of adjustment. Schooling, which is a protective factor in the life of a child when successful, does not function in that way for many foster children because of high rates of non-attendance and exclusion.

Particularly invidious for foster children who are taken into care (so often) because of maltreatment, is that they are seven to eight times more likely to be physically or sexually abused by their 'carers' compared with children in the general population. Sexual and physical maltreatment often occurs during home visits. The peer group is also likely (given their histories) to contain abusers. The short- and long-term adverse effects of sexual predation cannot be over-estimated.

Fostering sub-systems

Foster care involves the dynamic working of a social system with several sub-systems, for example:

■ birth parent–child (see below the sections on attachment and separation);

■ birth parent–social worker;

■ social worker–child;

■ social worker–foster parent;

■ birth parent–foster parent;

■ foster parent–foster child.

The foster parent–foster child relationship in the foster care system is pivotal, and on its success rests the justification of the fostering system.

Attributes of foster parents

Motivation has not proved a reliable predictor of future performance as a foster parent; indeed, a highly motivated carer can prove to be ineffectual. There is evidence that successful fostering depends upon the carer having open, flexible and reasonable expectations of the child. The *Foster Parent Attitude Scale* generated three significant factors:

1 *Achievement*: A desire to overcome obstacles, exert power, and strive to do something difficult as well and as quickly as possible.

2 *Nurturance*: An urge to nourish, help and protect the child.

3 *Play*: An ability to relax and have fun.

Fathers play a more active role in the foster children's lives than they are often given credit for. Foster parents' satisfactions in what they do are not dissimilar to the pleasures derived from their own children and grandchildren. For example:

- enjoying foster children's companionship;

- observing their progress;

- applying their parenting skills to facilitate their recovery from unhappy, possibly tragic, early experiences.

The needs of foster parents

Many foster parents, despite admirable attributes of patience and tolerance, plus outstanding care-giving and behaviour management skills, are overwhelmed by the problems of some of the children placed with them. Maltreatment, neglect and rejection may leave psychological 'scars' that express themselves in withdrawn ('emotionally frozen'), sexually inappropriate, violent and other deviant behaviours. Children with genetic and other physical disorders may present multiple impairments which are beyond the physical and emotional resources of the foster parents. The preparation and support of foster parents are too often inadequate.

▶ The break-up of children's families

The reasons for the placement of children in foster homes arise from parents being incarcerated for crimes, for physical, sexual or emotional abuse of the child or adolescent, domestic violence, the child being out of parental control, to mention a few possibilities. Although separations may not be so due to the break-up of family life through divorce and separation, the reactions of the child are likely to show similarities. In the Wallerstein and Kelly (1980) studies it was clear that children responded to the break-up of their homes in different ways, according to their ages. An examination of the characteristic reactions and behavioural changes revealed that:

- young pre-school children (aged $2\frac{1}{2}-3\frac{1}{4}$ years) tended to manifest regressive behaviour;

- middle pre-school children (aged $3\frac{3}{4}-4\frac{3}{4}$ years) showed irritability, aggressive behaviour, self-blame and bewilderment;

- older pre-school children (aged 5–6 years) displayed increased anxiety and aggressive behaviour;

distressed. 'Therapeutic' parenting (i.e. tender, loving care) from foster parents may be precisely what is needed for these children. Research suggests that where residential care is often detrimental to children's mental health, foster care may improve it. There is, of course, a threshold of psychopathological symptoms above which professional help is unavoidable.

Foster parents need help in developing therapeutic skills for working with children in their care who are 'disturbed' (see the foster parents' training programme in Chapter Nine). A framework of attachment theory is required to assess the therapeutic needs of foster children, and in particular their need for security of attachment, before they can engage in other therapeutic approaches successfully. The reasons why these children form dysfunctional attachment relationships require exploration before working to develop secure attachments between them and their carers. Attachment theory is discussed in a separate section later in this chapter.

Successful adaptation, no matter what life crisis is faced by an individual child, is dependent upon discovering new adaptive behaviours to meet changing circumstances. Looked-after children can be remarkably resilient, but many are so damaged by neglect and abuse that they are very vulnerable. Some defend themselves with an air of indifference, emotional frozenness, attention-seeking, or a generally hostile attitude to all and sundry. Foster parents' understanding of the typical reactions to major transitional events could help children to create new 'stories' (schemata) about themselves and their lives, and about the processes of change 'submerging' them – a process called 'reframing' or 'cognitive restructuring'. The typical (although not invariable) cycle of reaction to transitional trauma involves:

- *Immobilisation*: Initially the child (or adult) may feel overwhelmed, unable to make plans, or finding it difficult to comprehend or respond reasonably to what has happened. Many report the experience of this phase as a feeling of being frozen, paralysed or numb.

- *Minimisation*: In the second phase the child/adult may make light of events, even to the point of trivialising them. Individuals often deny that change has taken place. Denial provides time for a temporary retreat from reality. It allows children to regroup their internal 'forces' while finding the strength to comprehend the new life (e.g. the loss of a parent or entire family; their impending adoption) that the separation or some other trauma has forced upon them. Generally, intense pain and grief accompany this transition.

- *Depression*: Eventually, for most children, the reality of the changes in their lives becomes increasingly inescapable. In this phase there is a growing awareness that some alterations in the way the youngster is living are inevitable; this breakthrough of reality (if it comes) is sometimes accompanied by depression. The depression is usually the consequence of feeling powerless, and sensing that one's life is 'diminished' or out of one's control. Some individuals become so intensely depressed that they entertain suicidal ideas.

- *Letting go*: As children become more aware of the realities, they are generally able to progress to the point of actually accepting the new reality for what it is. This is where sensitive, consistent fostering can prove so crucial. In the first three phases there was an attachment to the past or pre-transitional situation – whether conscious or not. The move to the fourth phase involves a process of disengagement from the past and of being able to say, 'Here I am now; here is what I have; I know I can survive.' As the new reality dawns, optimism becomes possible. What is crucial is a process of 'letting go'. The troubling question is: 'Will there be another traumatic change around the corner?'

Rules and regulations

This is not the place to discuss the legal and administrative background to fostering. Suffice it to say that children who are looked after in foster homes are subject to regulations intended to safeguard their welfare by setting out minimum requirements for (*inter alia*) social work supervision and for medical care. In practice, as many foster parents tell us in the course of our research studies, the regulations are at times frustrating – even counter-productive – in coping with children who are often highly disruptive. There are 'ship's lawyers' among some foster children who are capable of manipulating, even intimidating, their carers. This may be part of a general pattern of non-conformist behaviour that also shows itself at school. It may be part of a 'survival' strategy that maintains the child's sense of being a real and independent person.

The issues of emotional and other support for hard-pressed foster care staff, and protection for looked-after children, are important ones, requiring high levels of liaison, support and supervision, between Social Services and the foster parents.

Protective factors

In general, the best predictor for a good long-term outcome is a child's ability to form at least one good and crucial relationship, not necessarily with a parent or relation. Education also protects the mental health of high-risk children. Life satisfaction for ex-foster care children is associated with having qualifications, a job and a partner. At the policy level, earlier admission to long-term foster care and later discharge are associated with a better outcome for children, as is the absence of conduct problems.

Users' views

It is very easy to disregard or ignore the actual experience of those receiving services. Agencies are inclined to disempower clients in the face of pressure to manage the limited resources available to deal with complex problems. The views of foster carers, residential carers, children and young people who are fostered, and care-leavers (regarding the support and interventions they feel they need) should always be sought. An analysis of the *National Child Development Study, 1958–91* (Bullen, 2002) data showed that children in care (it was not possible because of changes in practice and policy to distinguish between different types of care) were:

■ less satisfied with their lives as 16-year-olds, and

■ significantly more at risk of depression at 33 years of age.

Despite the gloomy findings above, 75 per cent of 16-year-olds and 80 per cent of the 33-year-olds did not have psychological problems. Following an extensive review of (*inter alia*) the longer-term outcomes of being looked after, Rushton and Minnis (2002, p. 366) conclude a comprehensive review of the fostering literature by observing that 'considering the levels of emotional and behavioural problems noted in childhood, studies of ex-foster children adults, as a whole, give a surprisingly positive picture'.

▶ ## The concept of attachment

An important question in the lives of foster children, and a matter of concern to their carers, is the nature of the emotional attachments they develop early on, and the extent to which new ones should or should not be encouraged while in care. Attachment refers to the tie between two or more individuals; it is a psychological relationship which is discriminating and specific and which bonds one to the other in space and over enduring periods of time. Researchers and clinicians have been particularly concerned with two types of attachment: parental attachment and infantile attachment.

Infantile and maternal attachments

The specific attachment of a young being to a particular adult or adult-substitute is known as *infantile attachment*. Just as an infant becomes attached to its mother, so also a mother develops a bond with her infant – a type of attachment known as *maternal bonding*. The most influential writings have been those of John Bowlby. His early view (1969, 1973) was that the child's strong attachment to its mother was essential for normal, healthy development, and, conversely, that deprivation of maternal affection or protracted maternal separation were liable to result in maladjustment which could show itself in a variety of ways, including delinquency. Bowlby's later view (1988), following an examination of further research findings, was that the child's separation from its care-giver did not inevitably result in the maladjustment of the child. Nevertheless, a long-lasting absence of a mother-figure before the age of about five years (in the absence of stable high-quality care) can compromise the child's healthy psychological development.

Mother–child symmetry

Bowlby points to the survival value of systems that ensure close proximity and contact between infant and mother during the long period of human immaturity. The young baby's crying is one of five *in-built* signals (crying, smiling, sucking, following and clinging) which, given the appropriate reaction of the mother, ensure physical closeness. His notion of the sensitive mother assumes a neat symmetry between the needs of the baby and the activity of the mother. Not only is the baby's behaviour 'built in'; the mother is seen as genetically programmed to respond to his or her signals. The mother is 'biologically attuned' as a member of the same species. Maternal sensitivity is thought to be critical for the development of a stable and happy relationship.

Foster carers' personal feelings may be challenged. They question how 'bonded' to another person's child – someone who may move on at any time – they can allow themselves to become, even if it were a matter entirely within their conscious choice. There is no simple answer to this dilemma. For John Bowlby (1969) and Mary Ainsworth (Ainsworth et al., 1978), the ability to use an attachment figure as a secure base provides a haven of safety and the confidence necessary for the child to explore and master everyday environments. Ainsworth and her colleagues (1978) designed a 'strange situation' experimental method to test infants' attachment behaviour:

A mother enters a room with her infant.

Some minutes later a stranger enters too.

After a few minutes the mother departs quietly, leaving her baby alone with the stranger.

The mother then returns and the stranger leaves the room.

It was possible to identify four distinct styles of attachment:

1 The 'securely attached' infant reacted positively to the stranger when the mother was present, but was visibly fearful and cried when she left. When she returned, the distressed infant went to her and was speedily comforted.

2 The 'insecure/avoidant' infants were somewhat indifferent to their mother when she was in the room, and they may or may not have expressed distress when she left. When she returned, they made no move to interact with her, stiffened or looked away.

3 The 'insecure/ambivalent' infants were distressed on entering the room and showed little exploration. They were very distressed when the mother left. When she returned they wished to be near her, but resisted all her efforts to comfort them. They struggled if picked up, and showed a great deal of angry behaviour.

4 The 'disorganised' infant showed incomplete, interrupted movements, and freezing. There was fear of the parent. The main feature was the lack of a coherent attachment strategy.

Ainsworth's findings suggest that:

- Maternal sensitivity is influential in determining the child's reactions.

- Sensitive mothering was exhibited towards the infant's behaviour in the homes of the securely attached infants.

- Insecurely attached, anxious and avoidant infants were found to have their interactive behaviour rejected by the mothers.

- In the case of the insecurely attached, anxious and resistant infants, a disharmonious and often ambivalent mother–infant relationship was evident. The resistant and ambivalent behaviours shown resulted from inconsistent parenting.

Research indicates that insecure attachments can be remedied and that a positive bond with one parent can compensate for a poor relationship with the other. Attachments to 'significant' adults outside the family such as teachers and (if looked after) foster parents, also play a part in protecting children against adverse outcomes associated with continuing insecurity, for example, poor mental health or educational under-achievement. These findings, in turn, contribute to the case for family support services, including parenting and foster parenting programmes.

What defines attachment?

Proximity seeking (for example, following) is commonly interpreted as an index of infant–parent attachment; other indicators include behaviour in 'strange situations' and activities such as differential smiling, crying and vocalisation, as well as protest at separation. Multiple criteria are used to specify attachment phenomena because of individual differences in the way attachment is organised and manifested – differences that seem to be related to variations among mothers in their infant-care practices. Indeed, because the child's attachment system is, in a sense, the reciprocal of that of the parents, it may be preferable to speak of, say, the mother and young child as forming a single, superordinate attachment system. It takes two to form a relationship! We are dealing with an 'attachment system' – an interacting couple – *not* simply a mother's feelings or a baby's feelings. The delicate and complementary intermeshing of their respective, individual attachment repertoires is such that it is not possible to describe one fully without also describing the other. Both must be considered in arriving at judgements of attachment.

A mother's actions speak louder than her rhetoric. She is 'bonded' if she looks after her infant well, demonstrating awareness of his or her needs by responding to them promptly and consistently. Mother–infant attachment is usually inferred, in the scientific literature on bonding, from *observations* of considerable and considerate attention to the child, demonstrating her love by smiling, vocalising, touching, kissing, cuddling, and prolonged gazing. Sequences of mother–child interactive behaviours are likely to provide a better indication of the parent–infant relationship than a one-sided account. The notion of a dialogue (or 'conversation') between two individuals has been used as an indicator of the quality of attachments and gives rise to a definition of 'good' relationships expressed in terms of the reciprocity of interactions between the partners. 'Good' mothers are responsive to their babies and continue to respond until they are satisfied; they also initiate activities. Figures 2.1a and b provide examples of questionnaires designed to explore attachment behaviour in mothers.

The markers for an absence of bonding might be maternal reports of detachment, indifference or hostility towards the baby, and of having a sense of the child being a 'stranger' or separate from her or him emotionally.

Child's name: _____ Child's age: _____

Caregiver's name: _____ Date: _____

---

1. When did you feel that your baby really belonged to you?
Immediately he or she was born ☐
The feeling developed over the first few days ☐
The feeling developed over the first year ☐
I still feel that he or she is a bit of a stranger ☐
I feel that he or she is a stranger. I have never felt that he or she belongs to me. ☐

---

2. Did anything happen to you to make you feel the baby really belonged to you or was part of you?
YES ☐
NO ☐
What happened? _____ DON'T KNOW ☐
_____

---

3. Do you have time to play with your child?
NEVER ☐
SELDOM ☐
SOMETIMES ☐
OFTEN ☐

---

4. Do you enjoy playing with your child?
NEVER ☐
SELDOM ☐
SOMETIMES ☐
USUALLY ☐

---

5. Does your child give you a lot of pleasure?
NEVER ☐
SOMETIMES ☐
OFTEN ☐
ALWAYS ☐

---

6. Is your child worth all you have had to give up?
YES ☐
NO ☐
DON'T KNOW ☐

---

7. Do you feel resentful towards your child?
NEVER ☐
SELDOM ☐
OFTEN ☐
ALWAYS ☐

Figure 2.1a Attachment questionnaire. [This form to be completed by the Caregiver.]

| Child's name: _____ | Child's age: _____ |
| Caseworker's name: _____ | Date: _____ |

Observations

Does the parent do any of the following?	YES	NO	CANNOT SAY
Initiate positive interactions with the infant?			
Respond to the infant's vocalizations?			
Change voice tone when talking to the infant?			
Show interest in face-to-face contact with the infant?			
Show the ability to console or comfort the infant?			
Enjoy close physical contact with the infant?			
Respond to the infant's indications of distress?			

Figure 2.1b Parent–infant attachment (bonding). [This form to be completed by the Caseworker.]

▶ Conclusion

The term 'looked-after children', which replaced 'foster children', is applied to children in the care of local authorities in England and Wales. They spend brief and longer-term periods in care interspersed with periods in what are often less than favourable own-home environments. Some children may get regular visits from birth parents, have irregular contacts, or get none at all. Arrangements for 'looked-after' children and adolescents break down to a worrying extent, usually within about a year. Behaviour and emotional problems are significantly correlated with the breakdown of placements. The interventions effective in reducing such problems in looked-after children are those carried out either in close liaison with foster carers, or directly through foster carers. They are, after all, usually the stable figures in the child's life. With appropriate support and training, they can make a real difference to children's lives.

▶ Select bibliography

Ainsworth, M.D., Behar, M., Waters, E. and Wall, S. (1978) *Patterns of Attachment*. Hillsdale, NJ: Lawrence Erlbaum.

Bowlby, J. (1969) *Attachment and Loss*. Vol. 1. London: Hogarth Press.

Bowlby, J. (1973) *Attachment and Loss*. Vol. 2. New York: Basic Books.

Bowlby, J. (1988) *Attachment and Loss*. Vol. 3. New York: Basic Books.

Browne, K. and Herbert, M. (1998) *Preventing Family Violence*. Chichester: Wiley.

Bullen, N. (2002) *National Child Development Study, 1958–1991* (SN.3148 2nd edn). London: MIMAS.

Chess, S. and Thomas, A. (1995) *Temperament in Clinical Practice*. New York: Guilford Press.

Department of Health (1998) *Prevalence of Specific Child and Adolescent Mental Health Problems*. London: Department of Health.

Farrington, D. (1995) The Twelfth Jack Tizard Memorial Lecture: The development of offending behaviour from childhood. *Journal of Child Psychology and Psychiatry*, 36, 929–964.

Forehand, R. and McMahon, R. (1981) *Helping the Noncompliant Child: A Clinician's Guide to Parent Training*. New York: Guilford Press.

Hayner, S.N. and O'Brien, W.H. (1990) Functional analysis in behavior therapy. *Clinical Psychology Review*, 10, 649–668.

Herbert, M. (1993) *Working with Children and the Children Act*. Leicester: BPS Books.

Herbert, M. (2002). Behavioural therapies. In M. Rutter and E. Taylor (eds) *Child and Adolescent Psychiatry*. Oxford: Blackwell Science.

Herbert, M. (2003) *Typical and Atypical Development: From Conception to Adolescence*. Oxford: BPS Blackwell.

Herbert, M., Sluckin, W. and Sluckin, A. (1983) Mother-to-infant bonding. *Journal of Child Psychology and Psychiatry*, 23, 205–221.

Hobbs, G., Hobbs, C. and Wynne, J. (1999) Abuse of children in foster care and residential care. *Child Abuse and Neglect*, 23, 1239–1252.

Iwaniec, D., Herbert, M. and Sluckin, A. (1988) Helping emotionally abused children who fail to thrive. In K. Brown, C. Davies and P. Stratton (eds) *Early Prediction and Prevention of Child Abuse*. Chichester: Wiley.

Kazdin, A.E. (1998) Psychosocial treatments for conduct disorder in children. In P. Nathan and J. Gorman (eds) *A Guide to Treatments That Work*. New York: Oxford University Press.

Loeber, R. and Hay, D.F. (1997) Key issues in the development of aggression and violence from childhood to early adulthood. *Annual Review of Psychology*, 48, 371–410.

Meltzer, H., Garwood, R., et al. (2000) *The Mental Health of Children and Adolescents in Great Britain*. London: Office of National Statistics.

Patterson, G. (1982) *Coercive Family Process*. Eugene, OR: Castalia.

Quinton, D., Rushton, H., Dance, C. and Mayes, D. (1998) *Joining New Families*. Chichester: Wiley.

Rushton, A. and Mayes, D. (1997) Forming fresh attachments in childhood: a research update. *Child and Family Social Work*, 2, 121–127.

Rushton, A. and Minnis, H. (2002) Residential and foster family care. In M. Rutter and E. Taylor (eds) *Child and Adolescent Psychiatry*, Oxford: Blackwell Science.

Rutter, M. (1985) Resilience in the face of adversity: protective factors and resistance to psychiatric disorder. *British Journal of Psychiatry*, 147, 589–611.

Sturmey, P. (1996) *Functional Analysis in Clinical Psychology*. Chichester: Wiley.

Taylor, E. (1994) *The Hyperactive Child: A Parents' Guide*. London: Optima.

Taylor, T.K. and Biglan, A. (1998) Behavioral family interventions for improving child-rearing: a review of the literature for clinicians and policy makers. *Clinical Child and Family Psychology Review*, 1, 41–60.

Wahler, R.G. and Meginnis, K.L. (1997) Strengthening child compliance through positive parenting practices: what works? *Journal of Clinical Child Psychology*, 26, 433–440.

Wallerstein, J. and Kelly, J. (1980) *Surviving the Breakup: How Children and Parents Cope with Divorce*. New York: Basic Books.

Webster-Stratton, C. and Herbert, M. (1994) *Troubled Families: Problem Children. Working with Parents: A Collaborative Process*. Chichester: Wiley.

CHAPTER THREE

Disruption in the classroom

▶ Introduction

There is significant empirical evidence to indicate that work with parents plays a crucial role in helping to overcome emotional and behavioural problems among school pupils of all ages. British educators commonly use the term *Emotional and Behavioural Difficulties* (EBD) as an umbrella term to describe a wide range of individual, social and personal difficulties which include activities that interfere with or disrupt the endeavours of others engaged in an organised group (e.g. a classroom of pupils). They interrupt, shout, tease, talk at the wrong time, get out of their seats, pester, disobey, and fight. Between 10 per cent and 20 per cent of all school-age children manifest these difficulties. Attention Deficit Hyperactivity Disorder (AD/HD) is a common EBD problem.

The use of behavioural methods to manage disruptive behaviour in the classroom is most effective when linked to reinforcement originating in the child's home. Research evidence indicates that schools are most effective when staff, pupils and pupils' families work cooperatively toward the same negotiated goals. These goals are very much a determinant of the school's organisation and management.

▶ The influence of school life

Schools are in a powerful position to exert influence on their students – children and adolescents – because they provide a work and play environment for nearly a dozen years during a formative period of development. Children spend almost as much of their waking life at school as at home. And it is not only an influence in terms of the transmission of academic, technical skills and cultural interests. The school introduces boys and girls to social and working relationships and to various forms of authority which they would not experience in the family. The areas of particular influence – academic success, social behaviour, moral values and occupational choice – represent major themes in the socialisation of young people.

There is no doubt that it does matter which school a pupil attends; certain features of the school curriculum and social ethos are of vital importance to its young pupils. Many parents will not be surprised to hear that research confirms the assumptions they make in trying desperately to get their offspring into a 'good' school. Adolescents are more likely to show socially acceptable behaviour and good scholastic attainment if they attend certain schools rather than others.

If youngsters, in general, find schoolwork interesting and relevant, they are likely to present few problems such as inattention, poor attainment and disruptive activities. However, failure in a world (particularly in a school with high academic aspirations) orientated toward success has significant consequences for the self-esteem of children, not only in the classroom, but also in other aspects of their lives. A sense of failure often manifests itself in a façade of rebellious disruption behind which children escape and deny reality. School is the place where confrontation with society is likely to take root for children who are unwilling or unable to learn.

▶ The consultation (triadic) model

A significant approach to classroom disruption involves the *triadic* model of providing consultations or workshops/courses for teachers and parents separately or together. The assumption is that as they are *in situ* most of the time, they are the people best placed to bring about behavioural change in disruptive children and, indeed, in some of their own interactions with them. The strategic approach to successful classroom management is based on applied Social Learning Theory; the tactics of discipline are drawn from cognitive-behavioural techniques.

Effective intervention strategies need to encompass the whole school. Outcomes that require temporal and situational generalisation have to go beyond social and cognitive behaviour management programmes to the level of organisational, practical and collaborative strategies. These are discussed below.

Context: the school as an organisation

Researchers have demonstrated that the prevalence of disturbance and disruption in schools is systematically related to their organisational characteristics. Differences in the way schools 'perform' are not due to the state of the buildings, the age or size of the school, even when physical factors seem unpromising. Rather, they owe their favourable outcomes to their attributes as *social institutions*. Part of the answer to motivating children lies in organising the school and its curriculum in a manner that is responsive to their needs and is fair and purposeful, but not patronising. The school that does well with examination results also does well on social measures (e.g. low delinquency rates and low truancy rates). The school's atmosphere, if benign, encourages positive social and academic responses from pupils.

This is not the place to discuss structural causes of school success and failure; rather, the issue is the behaviour of teachers and its influence in achieving cooperative, on-task, and appropriate classroom behaviour from pupils.

Context: the teacher in the classroom

The teacher is the key to children's happiness and productivity at school and notably the efficiency with which they learn. Twelve-year-olds who were questioned in a London study (Moore, 1966) (carried out in the 1960s) regarded the schools they had attended primarily in terms of how the teachers had treated them. The children appreciated teachers who were helpful, gave clear explanations, and kept order with fairness, humour, kindliness and good manners. They resented anything they saw as unfair, shouting, ranting and grumbling in the class, confusing instructions, boring teaching, physical punishment and, most of all, the humiliation of individual pupils.

Contemporary students also have very clear ideas about what offends their dignity, self-respect and self-esteem. This is due to teachers who:

- interpret their role too literally and rigidly;
- treat students as anonymous entities or as members of a horde rather than as individuals;
- seem to lack humanity;
- are too straight-laced;
- are 'soft' and cannot keep control;
- are inconsistent;
- are unfair/unjust.

▶ Classroom management

Solving disciplinary problems demands a curriculum that satisfies pupils' needs. To do well in school, children need to feel and believe they can be successful and recognise that they are cared about by their teachers.

Favourable ('good teacher') outcomes are related to the following:

- actions in lessons (e.g. the way teachers talk to students; maintain an air of quiet authority; appear just; make 'rewards' and incentives available; refrain from shouting at and ridiculing students);
- the creation of 'good' conditions for students (e.g. a sense of being treated fairly; of having a varied and interesting curriculum; an expectation that students are at school to learn; a pride in good standards);
- the provision of opportunities for students to take on responsibility;
- an emphasis on teachers getting to know the students in the class and having the insight to understand the reasons that underlie many of their actions;
- the ability of teachers to anticipate likely control problems, to nip them in the bud, and respond promptly, effectively and consistently;
- a classroom environment that is welcoming, colourful and stimulating;

- teachers who avoid unnecessary or impractical threats;
- teachers who are able to enjoy a 'laugh' *with* students;
- teachers who can generate warm, friendly relationships;
- teachers who treat students with respect;
- a degree of freedom being allowed to students.

Models of discipline

The phrase 'catch the child out in good behaviour, not only bad behaviour', so valuable for managing children at home, also has a significant place in the school environment. The amount of formal punishment applied in the classroom makes little difference in producing 'good behaviour'. In fact, too frequent disciplinary interventions are actually associated with an increase in disruptive activity. Demeaning activities such as sarcasm, ridicule and shouting are notorious for militating against positive educational objectives; they tend to exacerbate misbehaviour and increase alienation from school authority. There are parallels here with parental discipline.

An authoritarian approach to behaviour management in the classroom is the least effective of various disciplinary models. The most successful method makes use of dynamic group processes, and the teacher's ability to develop a supportive social/emotional climate in the classroom. An effective disciplinary procedure must do the following:

- work to stop disruptive behaviour and/or increase appropriate behaviour;
- be a method acceptable to the teacher;
- be geared toward teaching the child a better decision-making process;
- be modelled by the teacher;
- be understood by all involved;
- be consistent with the principles of effective discipline.

These methods, in turn, require the provision of:

- effective teaching practices;
- subjects that stimulate interest and motivate children;
- interventions that meet children's basic needs;
- opportunities offered in the classroom to express stress in appropriate ways;
- rules and consequences that are developed collaboratively with students;
- teaching and modelling of active and effective communication skills.

These preventive proactive strategies should minimise conflicts between children and teachers.

▶ Disruptive behaviour

There are several causes of disruptive behaviour in the classroom, such as attention problems or AD/HD. But not all classroom disruption can be blamed on children with clinical disorders. Problems of classroom control have many and varied causes. Nevertheless, children with *Oppositional Defiant Disorder* (ODD) or *Conduct Disorder* (CD) are undoubtedly capable of making life difficult and, sometimes, unsupportable for teachers. Behaviour that is disruptive at school tends to occur in particular situations between:

- pupil and authority (lateness, absenteeism, abuse, non-compliance, off-task activity);

- pupil and work (repeated failure to do homework or produce written assignments);

- pupil and teacher (abusive language, physical assault, persistent interruptions, disruption of classmates);

- pupil and pupil (bullying, intimidation, extortion, theft).

Interventions: contingency management

The contingency principle is one of the lynchpins of effective behavioural interventions to change children's behaviour, and is detailed in the standard Child-Wise behaviour management programme in Chapter Six. Perhaps the most obvious and natural reinforcement available to the teacher is the attention given to their pupils, in the form of a smile, words of encouragement, or even mere proximity. Adult attention is a powerful secondary reinforcer for the child acquired over the years by an association between adult attention and the provision of primary reinforcers such as food, security, comfort and affection. Teacher attention tends to increase those behaviours that attracted it in the first place. When teachers pay attention to pupils who are on-task and working well, such activity tends to be strengthened. The converse also applies: paying attention to minor infringements increases their frequency. Unfortunately, given the potency of the 'contingency principle' (the systematic application and/or withdrawal of reinforcement), teachers generally find fault more than they praise. Given the adverse circumstances in the lives of many children with disruptive conduct disorders (e.g. rejection, maltreatment, insecurity and separations), it is not surprising if adult attention does not necessarily prove particularly reinforcing for all children.

Self-defeating practices usually go unnoticed by those who use them because they only see the immediate results, but rarely assess the full or long-term effects their behaviour may have on others. These interactions are unwittingly set in motion and maintained because ineffective short-term control techniques are reinforced in the users by their success. This success is more apparent than real; there is only a *temporary* suppression of deviant behaviour. The teachers have rewarded annoying conduct in students who, in turn, have rewarded the teacher's shouting by their momentary compliance; the net effect is that both kinds of performance are mutually escalated.

Contingency management programmes

The early use of token systems for modifying classroom behaviour such as the Good Behaviour Game and Class or Recess have enjoyed short-term successes but do not generalise over longer periods of time in the youngster's life at school. Hard-pressed teachers have great difficulty implementing complicated and time-consuming behaviourally based programmes – especially as only a relatively small minority of the pupils in classrooms (other than in special units) present seriously disruptive behaviour. Later developments of classroom programmes – psycho-educational, behavioural and cognitive – have been numerous, diverse in nature, but only moderately effective.

Attention Deficit Hyperactivity Disorder (AD/HD)

Children who are hyperactive are in many ways a special case. They are the cause of frequent complaints at school. *Attention Deficit Hyperactivity Disorder* (AD/HD) is estimated to occur in as many as 3 to 6 per cent of school-age children. They can be so disruptive that they may be referred to a professional by teachers who despair at being unable to manage them, or to teach them owing to their poor attention.

Hyperactive children may be difficult to define, but their nomadic wilful style in the classroom is very recognisable. For school-based observations Claire Jones (1994) provides observational questions for the teacher as follows:

- Does the child impulsively answer questions (or select answers in forced-choice formats) without appearing to think about alternatives?

- Does the child fidget even when appearing interested in the task?

- Does the child's conversation appear random, or sound like a 'free flight of ideas'?

- Does the child look away from the task in response to noises or visual distractions?

- Does the child comment on external noises or objects in the room that are unrelated to the task at hand?

- Does the child frequently ask questions such as 'When will this be over?', 'What's next?' or 'What other things can we do?'

- Does the child yawn after activities requiring sustained attention?

- Does the child doodle in class or draw on hands, clothing, and other things?

- Does the child stare off into space or appear to be 'glass-eyed'?

- Does the child lose papers, assignments, books, and the like?

- Are the child's desk and backpack messy and disorganised?
- Is the child able to stay alert during tasks requiring sustained attention?
- Does the child appear to lack persistence?

The attentional component

Some children have attention problems but are not hyperactive; some indeed are slow and lethargic, and less impulsive or aggressive than AD/HD children. Hyperactivity makes up one component either singly, or in combination with difficulties in concentrating (attentional) – hence 'Attention Deficit Hyperactivity Disorder'. Many factors will affect how well a child attends: the type of activity, what has preceded the activity throughout the child's day, and the child's level of interest in the task. Children often daydream or become preoccupied with intrusive worries when emotionally disturbed by distressing life events – an 'off-task' activity that annoys teachers.

It is estimated that a developmentally appropriate length of attention for a sustained attention activity, such as viewing television, is as follows:

2 years old: 7 minutes

3 years old: 9 minutes

4 years old: 13 minutes

5 years old: 15 minutes

6 to 7 years old: 60 minutes

These times are presented as guidelines only; children vary greatly in their attention spans. However, children with attention disorders will find it challenging to maintain attention on a structured task for these lengths of time.

Reframing (cognitive restructuring)

Reframing is a useful technique for maintaining a degree of calm when coping with a child with AD/HD. Reframing is an alteration in the emotional or conceptual viewpoint in relation to which a situation is experienced. That experience is placed in another 'frame' which fits the facts of the situation as well (or more plausibly), thus transforming its entire meaning. Giving people different 'stories' to tell themselves about themselves or about events – stories that are less self-defeating or destructive – is a feature of cognitive-behavioural work. A constructive use of reframing might be with teachers who always tend to perceive the negative in (say) AD/HD children. To alter negative schemata or attributions, the teachers could reframe the child's behaviour as follows:

- what is described as distractible behaviour might be recast as alertness to what is going on;

- a distorted sense of time might indicate tirelessness when motivated;

- impatience could be seen as keenness to get on with things;

- out-of-seat activity might mean being energetic and lively;

- talking out of turn might be enthusiasm or keenness to contribute.

The method should not condone extreme or persistently inappropriate behaviour. It must be used judiciously and genuinely, and communicated to the pupil without sarcasm, in a manner that shows respect.

There is a conceptual difficulty for some teachers in whose attributions problematic behaviours are reified into entities which reside within the child ('There's a little demon in him'; 'He's always trying to get at me'; 'It's his bad home influence'). The teacher does not share, in any way, in the 'ownership' of the problem. Such a denial of any role in the child's negative behaviours can be risky for the child (punitive attitudes are encouraged); it is also very difficult to deal with in a classroom setting. It might be possible by means of reframing to modify such attributions – by encouraging teachers to make 'connections' ('Do you see anything of yourself at that age in your pupil's behaviour?'; 'Were you like the pupil at her age?'), and to think about behaviour sequentially and contingently (the ABC functional analysis, explained on pp. 46–48).

▶ Select bibliography

Barkley, R. (1995) *Taking Charge of ADHD: The Complete Authoritative Guide for Parents.* New York: Guilford Press.

Becker, W.C., Madsen, C.H., Arnold, C. and Thomas, D.R. (1967) The contingent use of teacher attention and praise in reducing classroom behavior problems. *Journal of Special Education,* 1, 287–307.

Braswell, L. and Bloomquist, M. (1991) *Cognitive Behavioural Therapy for ADHD Children: Child, Family and School Interventions.* New York: Guilford Press.

Brestan, E.V. and Eyberg, S.M. (1998) Effective psychosocial treatment of conduct-disordered children and adolescents: 29 years, 82 studies, 5275 children. *Journal of Clinical Child Psychology,* 27, 180–189.

Du Paul, G.J. and Stoner, G. (2003) *ADHD in the Schools: Assessment and Intervention Strategies,* 2nd edn. London: Guilford Press.

Fontana, D. (1986) *Classroom Control.* Leicester: BPS Books/Methuen.

Goldstein, S. (ed.) (1995) *Understanding and Managing Children's Classroom Behavior.* New York: Wiley.

Haynes, S.N. and O'Brien, W.H. (1990) Functional analysis in behavior therapy. *Clinical Psychology Review,* 10, 649–668.

Herbert, M. (1987) *Conduct Disorders of Childhood and Adolescence,* 2nd edn. Chichester: Wiley.

Herbert, M. (1998) *Clinical Child Psychology: Social Learning, Development and Behaviour,* 2nd edn. Chichester: Wiley.

Jones, C. (1994) *Attention Deficit Disorder: Strategies for School-Age Children.* Tucson, AZ: Communication Skill Builders.

Loeber, R., Tremblay, R.E. et al. (1999) Continuity and desistance in disruptive boys' early fighting at school. *Development and Psychopathology,* 1, 39–50.

McCarthy, O. and Carr, A. (2002) Prevention of bullying. In A. Carr (ed) *Prevention: What Works with Children and Adolescents?* Hove: Brunner–Routledge.

Meltzer, H., Garwood, R. et al. (2000) *The Mental Health of Children and Adolescents in Great Britain*. London: Office of National Statistics.

Mendler, A.N. (1992) *What Do I Do When ...? How to Achieve Discipline with Dignity in the Classroom*. Bloomington, IN: National Education Service.

Moore, T. (1966) Difficulties of the ordinary child in adjusting to primary school. *Journal of Child Psychology and Psychiatry*, 2, 299–301.

O'Leary, K.D. and O'Leary S.G. (1977) *Classroom Management: The Use of Behavior Modification*, 2nd edn. Oxford: Pergamon Press.

Olweus, D. (1993) *Bullying in Schools: What We Know and What We Can Do*. Oxford: Blackwell.

Patterson, G. (1982) *Coercive Family Process*. Eugene, OR: Castalia.

Rutter, M. (1985) Resilience in the face of adversity: protective factors and resistance to psychiatric disorder. *British Journal of Psychiatry*, 147, 589–611.

Snowling, M.J. (1992) Reading and other learning difficulties. In M. Rutter and E. Taylor (Eds) *Child and Adolescent Psychiatry*. Oxford: Blackwell Science.

Sturmey, P. (1996) *Functional Analysis in Clinical Psychology*. Chichester: Wiley.

Taylor, E. (1994) *The Hyperactive Child: A Parents' Guide*. London: Optima.

Thomas, D.R., Becker, W.C. and Armstrong, B. (1968) Production and elimination of classroom disruptive behaviour by systematically varying teacher's behavior. *Journal of Applied Behavior Analysis*, 1, 35–45.

Walker, H.M. and Walker, J.E. (1991) *Coping with Non-Compliance in the Classroom*. Austin, TX: PRO-ED.

Walker, J.E. and Shea, T.M. (1991) *Behavior Management: A Practical Approach for Educators*. New York: Macmillan.

Webster-Stratton, C. and Herbert, M. (1994) *Troubled Families: Problem Children Working with Parents: A Collaborative Process*. Chichester: Wiley.

PART II

From theory to practice

Principles of assessment and training

CHAPTER FOUR

Behavioural parent training

▶ Introduction

It has been empirically established that restoring a balance of authority and control within the family (a problem referred to in Chapter One) is most effectively achieved by *triadic* behaviour management training (BMT) for parents. The BMT approach directly addresses the major conditions (e.g. failures of parenting and distortions of socialisation) that are known to contribute significantly to the development of childhood behaviour problems. If it is accepted that problematic behaviours of childhood are acquired largely as a function of faulty learning processes, then there is a case for arguing that certain problems can most effectively be modified where they occur by changing the 'social lessons' the child receives. Children can unlearn self-defeating behaviours; they can learn new, more advantageous ways of going about things; and in all of this, parents and teachers are generally the best people to help them achieve the necessary changes.

Parents use common-sense methods to rear their children, shaping and changing their behaviour in ways not too distant from the learning theory techniques of behaviour therapists. We claim that the basic *tactics* and *broad principles* of behaviour therapy (if not the theoretical small print, or ability to formulate strategically) are readily understood, and relatively straightforward to communicate to parents.

There are three key elements that produce effective outcomes in training courses for clinicians, social workers and health visitors: (1) behavioural theory; (2) assessment methods; and (3) behavioural methods (techniques).

▶ Behavioural theory

Learning and failures to learn are the keys to understanding the process of problem development. Behaviour results from a complex transaction between the individual child and a social environment that sometimes encourages and sometimes discourages certain actions. Rewards, punishments and other interactions are mediated by human beings and within attachment and social systems, and are not simply the impersonal consequences of behaviour. Children are relating to, interacting with, and learning from, people who have social and emotional meaning and value for them. They feel antipathetic to some, attached by respect

Practitioner Comment: There are times when it is judicious to turn a 'blind eye' to certain minor infringements (for example, accidents, temporary lapses of memory, and impulsive acts that constitute unimportant misdemeanours). The technique is useful when the child is playing up to manipulate you, showing unnecessary dependent behaviour, or to 'wind you up'. An example would be whining incessantly for your attention at an inappropriate time. There is nothing worse for actors than to remove their audience. So, as soon as the misbehaviour begins, turn away or walk away from your child; pretend not to see or hear what is going on; say nothing and try not to show any expression at all; resist getting into any debate, argument or discussion with your child while he or she is misbehaving. If you think your child deserves an explanation for whatever is upsetting him or her, then say, 'When you have calmed down, we will talk about it.'

If a child grabs toys or other goodies from his small brother, try to ensure that grabbing has no rewarding outcome. Return the toy to its owner. (You could combine the training that grabbing is unproductive with the teaching of *sharing* in the little one, and saying 'please'/waiting patiently in the older son. Encourage them to take turns.) Withhold reinforcements such as approval, attention and the like, which have previously and inappropriately followed unwanted behaviour. *Remember: your child may 'work hard' to regain the lost reinforcement and thus may get 'worse' before he or she gets 'better'.* If the problem behaviour has been continuously reinforced in the past, then reduction of an undesirable response (extinction) should be relatively swift; after all, it is much easier for the youngster to recognise that he or she has lost reinforcers than it is for the child on intermittent reinforcement. In the latter case, extinction tends to be slow.

Time-out

This procedure is intended to reduce ('extinguish') the frequency of an undesirable behaviour by ensuring that it is followed by a reduction in the opportunity to acquire reinforcement or rewards. In practice, one can distinguish two forms of time-out:

1 *Activity time-out* – where a child is simply barred from joining in an enjoyable activity, but still allowed to observe it – for example, having misbehaved, he or she is made to sit out of a game.

2 *Room time-out* – where he or she is removed from an enjoyable activity, not allowed to observe this, but not totally isolated – for example, standing outside in the hall having misbehaved.

Time-out sometimes leads to tantrums or rebellious behaviour such as crying, screaming and physical assaults, particularly if the child has to be taken by force to the end of the room (say, a 'naughty' chair). With older, physically resistive going to begin each session by reviewing the assignment from the previous week. If a parent fails to complete his or her homework, ask, for example: 'Were there difficulties that got in the way of doing the homework?'

It may be helpful to discuss at the outset the term 'homework' that is given to the essential tasks of practising new skills in 'real life' between sessions. Surveyed on this issue, most parents consider the word 'homework' appropriate, mainly because they like to feel they are attending a 'course' rather than therapy. A few parents thought the term patronising and too reminiscent of school days. The label 'practice sessions' could be an alternative if the objections are felt by a majority of the group.

▶ Resistance

Identify and discuss resistance

It is important not to overlook resistance to the course in general, and the discomfort of 'changing' in particular. Resistance can be reflected in persistent late arrival, obstructive ('disruptive') behaviour that hinders the participation of other group members, failing to do homework or to 'remember' to bring it to the session. It is here that it becomes crucial for others in the group to see how committed the leaders are in insisting politely on the rule about assignments. Figure 5.1 is helpful in defining the commitment to working toward change.

Anticipate potential difficulties. The philosophy of collaboration is not an argument for freedom to ignore the agreed terms of the contract for attending the course. However, the reluctant participant should not be 'put down' by accusing him/her of sophistry. Leaders might ask participants in advance to think about the difficulties they may encounter when they try to carry out the techniques they have just learned when at home (e.g. visitors, working late, a bad day, child unwell, and so on). Ask group members to let you know when unforeseen difficulties (a perennial problem for foster carers) arise. It may be worth mentioning as a potential advantage that when parents give their children attention for positive behaviours, they will gain more time for themselves in the long run. Their children are likely to cease behaving badly in order to get attention. (It's like a long-term investment!)

What is going wrong?

- Some parents have irredeemably negative attributions about the child, seeing no connection between their own actions and the child's behaviour, allowing them to blame him or her alone for everything.

- Parents might feel that their child must also change before they are willing to change.

| Child or Partner's name: | Child's age: |
| Caregiver's name: | Date: |

Tick the appropriate box

	AGREE	DISAGREE
I wish to do all I can to improve my relationship with him or her		
I want to know how to go about putting things right between us		
I need some assistance to sort things out for the better at home		
I accept that we *both* need to change		
The problems are not all on one side		
I hope that with an effort I can succeed		
We will both be happier if we can make changes		
I know it won't be easy to change but I intend to try		
I am ready to make an immediate change in my actions		
I know it will take time to make the necessary changes but accept it		
The past will have to be forgotten in order to make a good future		
I will not allow myself to be discouraged by the first setback		

Figure 5.1 Commitment to working toward change (in relationship with child and/or partner). [This form to be completed by the Caregiver.]

■ Others may have tried a particular approach in the past and found that it did not work.

■ Some may feel that the approach reminds them of something awful their parents did to them.

■ There may be a sense that the leaders are presenting simplistic answers to their child-rearing dilemmas and do not really understand their 'real-life' situations.

■ Not infrequently, participants may feel depressed and debilitated, and individual help and a suitable referral may be necessary.

■ Sometimes resistance is simply due to the parent not adequately understanding the concepts.

■ Another possibility is that the partners are resisting because they can't realistically complete the homework.

■ We should not forget that the leaders' *own* attitudes, insensitivities, or style may alienate the parents!

▶ Possible remedies to overcome resistance

It may be necessary to tailor the assignments to what the parents feel they can accomplish during the coming week, and tailor the leaders' behaviour if it is proving to be negative in its effects. Supervision should be helpful, especially if the leaders have a video of themselves at work.

Force field analysis

This method is useful for dealing with resistance when things become 'stuck', that is, when there is equilibrium between forces facilitating change and those that are opposing and restraining them. The process involves asking the parents to do the following:

- List facilitative or helping forces for change (e.g. a new, untried tactic, a renewal of determination to succeed, a restoring of confidence).

- List restraining or hindering forces for change (e.g. 'learned helplessness', exhaustion, never any respite from a demanding child, no leaving the house for outings).

- List alternative intervention strategies for: (1) strengthening existing facilitative forces, e.g. encouraging the mother to be more consistent by rewarding herself with a treat when successful; (2) adding new facilitative forces, e.g. an offer by a member of the group to baby-sit in order to give a mother a break or persuading a previously reluctant father to involve himself in the programme; and (3) weakening or removing restraining forces, e.g. debating away a member's inhibitions about being firm and decisive with their child.

- List the advantages and disadvantages of each intervention. Review areas of progress, which may have been forgotten within a 'global fog' of depression.

Ensure generalisation

Generalisation means teaching participants how to apply specific skills to deal with their current concerns, and also teaching them how to use those skills in other settings (e.g. the school or when shopping) or with new types of misbehaviour – problems that may occur in the future. Participating in group sessions is a powerful way to enhance generalisation because it exposes group members to a variety of family life situations and approaches to solving problems.

Predict relapses

Prepare parents for occasional setbacks, reassuring them that relapses are not unusual. Misjudgements about the best tactics and strategies may well occur. Life events (notably school holidays) can produce a relapse. The important point is to help participants find solutions to situations that seem 'blocked', and to withdraw from the therapeutic cul-de-sac by trying different tactics. It can be useful to rehearse what to do if this happens. In this situation it is useful to have the support of a parent from a previous course (helping in the group as a volunteer) who has overcome temporary setbacks by a mixture of perseverance and optimistic self-confidence. Another possibility is to arrange for some time-out (respite) from the children, to become 're-energised'.

No easy prescriptions

No 'pain' of hard work for parents in the short term means no 'gain' in improved behaviour in their children in the long term. Acknowledge that it is not easy to be a parent or to work with children, and that none of us were trained for the task. One of the most common misjudgements that adults make in relating to children is to go for the short-term payoffs (for example, to give in to a child's tantrum to stop the unpleasant behaviour) at the expenses of the long-term consequences (the child learns to have tantrums to get what he or she wants). The parenting skills presented in this manual take time to implement. It is a case of a far from easy 'investment' for the longer term that will pay more dividends than the seemingly 'easy' line of least resistance approach.

What about the hyperactive child? Children with AD/HD present special difficulties when their attention problems make them 'inaccessible' to the strategies their parents may be learning. The issue of the 'window of opportunity' offered by medication is discussed by Eric Taylor in his book on AD/HD (Taylor, 1997).

Reducing drop-out (attrition) rates

Primary attrition means that parents drop out before the course begins; secondary attrition means dropping out during the course. Both tend to be high in parent training groups. To mitigate the tendency to drop out, do the following:

- Elicit any possible fears parents may have about attending the course or talking in the group setting and arrange (with the agreement of the other participants) for them to be accompanied by a partner or close friend.

- Prepare the parents carefully by (preferably) visiting them at home, normalising their problem (many parents will be there with similar difficulties; all children can be problematic) *without* minimising it.

- If you are collecting data, do it during the course, rather than relying on parents to post it to you. Some may have difficulty with questionnaires and rating forms. Help them without seeming patronising.

- Negotiate a verbal or written agreement that emphasises mutual obligations and benefits.

- Emphasise diplomatically but firmly the importance of punctuality, regularity, and a group sense of comradeship and identity.

- Describe the essence of a collaborative mode of working.

- Send a welcoming/reminder card before the course begins.

- Find out about practical difficulties: transport, creche, persuading a partner to attend if possible, or to share knowledge/skills with (e.g. supply handouts/videos).

- Provide a creche with interesting toys; this is likely to enhance attendance as children are eager to attend and may chivvy a wavering parent.

- Give some written material as a reminder of the main purposes and procedures of the group.

- Make the group sessions fun. Have a laugh together. Humour is very important in behavioural parent training (BPT).

- Be warm and nurturant in style. Provide refreshments and share the waiter/waitress roles.

- Encourage a supportive attitude to each other (this usually surfaces early on and seldom requires prompting).

- Allow time for the all-important socialising and development of friendships.

- Be available during the mid-session break to hear about any personal difficulties or crises which parents might not be ready to share with other participants but which threaten future attendance or the quality of the homework observations/rehearsals.

- Phone the parent to find out why a session has been missed.

Literacy skills

The programme assumes that parents have basic literacy skills and that they are comfortable with general levels of discussion and debate. (If not, see the individual programme described in Chapter Seven.)

Parents with learning difficulties require programmes that are suitably modified to meet their conceptual and educational levels. There would, for example, be much greater emphasis on modelling parenting skills, and handouts need not be supplied. A possible alternative for written material would be the preparation of audio-tapes, or videos.

▶ Notes on the courses

1 Repetition: You will notice there is some overlap between the sessions in the courses. Repetition is important and necessary, hence the recurrence of themes and the reminders/précis/highlighting/summarising.

2 Home visits: If at all possible, arrange for a home visit to check whether parents can do what they have learned! (see the individual home-based programme described in Chapter seven).

3 Limits of confidentiality: Because the usual boundaries of individual patient confidentiality become somewhat blurred when participants in a group are sharing sometimes intimate information, you need to discuss with them where the boundaries lie in terms of (a) what participants talk about within and outside the group sessions; (b) where your responsibilities lie in relation to confidentiality with regard to individual disclosures in the group; and (c) your overriding duty to protect children should a child protection concern arise.

▶ Select bibliography

Achenbach, T.M. (1991) *Manual for the Child Behavior Checklist/4–18 and Profile*. Burlington, VT: Department of Psychiatry, University of Vermont.

Conners, C.K. (1997) *Conners' Rating Scales: Revised Technical Manual*. North Tornawanda, NY: Mental Health Systems.

Eyberg, S. and Pincus, D. (1999) *ECBI: Eyberg Child Behavior Inventory*. Odessa, FL: Psychological Assessment Resources.

Herbert, M. (1998) *Clinical Child Psychology: Social Learning, Development and Behaviour*, 2nd edn. Chichester: Wiley.

Taylor, E. (1997) *Understanding Your Hyperactive Child: The Essential Guide for Parents*. London: Vermilion.

Sergeant, J. and Taylor, E. (2002) Psychological testing and observation. In M. Rutter and E. Taylor (eds) *Child Psychology and Psychiatry*. Oxford: Blackwell Science.

Webster-Stratton, C. and Herbert, M. (1994) *Troubled Families: Problem Children. Working with Parents: A Collaborative Process*. Chichester: Wiley.

PART III

Courses

- Recording forms provided.
- Handout(s) given out.

Recap

Brief recap of core learning points.

Evaluation

Evaluation forms filled in/and collected.

Play assignment debriefing

- How many of the participants were able to find time to play with their child every day for 10 minutes? What makes it difficult to do this? What factors seemed to affect the quality of the play?
- What was the child's behaviour like during the play sessions?
- How did the play sessions affect the parent–child relationship?
- Did any of the parents dislike/find it very difficult to play?
- Was it due to lack of experience of playing in their own childhood, or because they felt uncomfortable in this role?
- Encourage these parents to invite their children to join them in tasks (e.g. baking, washing the car, arranging flowers).

▶ Session 4: Effective praise

See Appendix I.4 for the related handout.

Preliminaries
- Welcome.
- Résumé.
- Collect homework.

Homework
- Individual and group feedback.
- Discussion.

It's as simple as ABC (role play)
- The ABC of behaviour (the good behaviour rule).
- Parents' examples of ABC behaviour sequences at home.

- Encouraging desired behaviour. Continuous and intermittent reinforcement. Give examples.

See Appendix I.23 for the relevant ABC handout.

Buzz session (break)

How to praise

- Brainstorm (flip chart).
- Being specific (labelling praise).
- Invent situations for parents to role play praising their child.
- Discussion.

Suggestive praise

Examples of ways to praise, what to praise, when and how not to praise. Debate these issues.

Homework

- Praise your child for behaviours you like to see.
- Keep a record of some instances – how did you feel?; how did your child react?

Handouts

- Record sheet/praise.
- Activities for the week.
- Behaviour record.

Brief recap

Evaluation

Evaluation forms filled in and collected.

Homework prompts

'Special time' assignment

- How did you spend your special (quality) time with your child?
- Were there any difficulties?
- Did you enjoy the time? Did your child?

▶ Session 5: Tangible and social rewards

Preliminaries
- Welcome.
- Résumé: effective praise.
- Collect homework.

Homework
- Individual and group feedback.
- Discussion.

Rewards
- Rewards, privileges and incentives.
- Parents' childhood experiences of social and tangible rewards.
- Rewarding desired behaviour.
- Are they bribes?
- Discussion.

See Appendix I.14 for the relevant handout.

Buzz session (break)

Symbolic rewards

Brief discussion of rationale.

- Illustration of imaginative reward/sticker charts (see website).
- Brainstorm ideas for charts.

Homework

Design a behaviour (reward) chart with your child.

Handouts
- Guidelines.
- Behaviour recording forms (see Figure 6.3).
- Activities for the week.

Brief recap

Core learning points discussed.

Evaluation

Evaluation forms filled in and collected.

Behaviours I wish to see more of: **For using:**
                                              * **Praise (suggestive praise)**
                                              * **Tangible rewards**
                                              * **Symbolic rewards (stickers)**
                                              * **Noticing**

1. _____

2. _____

3. _____

4. _____

Behaviours I wish to see less of: **For using:**
                                              * **Ignoring**
                                              * **Time-out**
                                              * **Response cost**
                                              * **Logical consequence**

1. _____

2. _____

3. _____

4. _____

Figure 6.3   Behaviour record.

Homework prompts

Praise assignments

- How often do parents praise their children?

- Discuss some examples of the various ways parents praise their children.

▶ **Session 6: 'It's as simple as ABC!'**

B stands for Beliefs as well as Behaviour.

Preliminaries

- Welcome.
- Brief résumé.
- Collect homework.

Homework

Feedback.

Beliefs, thoughts and feelings

- The link between beliefs, thoughts, feelings and behaviour is explored.
- Exposition: the 'stories' parents tell themselves have an impact on the way they feel and the way they behave.
- On the flip chart, group members describe thoughts and feelings they have linked to their parenting abilities.
- The influence of culture and myths about the 'perfect parent'.
- How helpful or conflicting are the advice and attitudes of friends, relatives and neighbours?

Buzz session (break)

The ABC model of behaviour

- The cognitive-behavioural model is explained, i.e. the relationship between the *antecedent* (A) event or trigger, with the *belief* (B) used to interpret the event and the emotional *consequences* (C) (see Figure 6.4).
- Explanation (reminder) of how behaviour is acquired and reinforced.
- Importance of 'triggers' and setting events (times, persons, places and situations).

See Appendix 1.23 and www.wileyeurope.com/go/herbert for the relevant handout.

'Pay-offs'

The function of consequences or 'pay-offs' to children and parents. Examples given and asked for.

Evaluation

Handouts are provided and evaluation forms (Figures 6.4 and 6.5) filled in and collected.

Homework

Parents apply the theory at home. They use the handout, and the ABC recording chart (from the Wiley website) to break down a sequence of events into what led up to the child's misbehaviour and its consequences. It is important that they record their beliefs and feelings.

Child's name: _____	Child's age: _____
Caregiver's name: _____	Date: _____
	Week: _____

Time	Antecedent: what happened beforehand?	Belief: my feelings, attitudes, views at the time	Consequences: what happened next?	Distress rating 0–5 (see criteria below)

Rating criteria

```
0      1    2    3    4    5
|
No    LOW                VERY
distress              HIGH
         Level of distress felt
            during the episode
```

Figure 6.4   Caregiver ABC record chart. [This form to be completed by the Caregiver.]

Homework debriefing

View designed reward/sticker charts.

▶ **Session 7: Discipline**

Preliminaries

- Welcome.
- Brief résumé.
- Collect homework.

An illustration of a typical sequence

1. *Antecedent events* (possible precipitants)
Peter is asked to do something or to stop doing it.

2. *Behaviour*

(a) Non-compliance.
He takes no notice; if Mother insists, he resorts to verbal abuse.

(b) Verbal abuse.
He makes rude comments, criticises, occasionally swears and shouts.

Persons:	He's rude and disobedient, mainly with Mother; occasionally to Father; never with Grandmother.
Places:	Anywhere.
Times:	Meals in particular – at the beginning, usually, of the family meal.
Situations:	Mainly when asked to do something or when challenged over being late for meals or for bad manners. Particularly when questioned about, or criticised for not eating properly, getting up and leaving the table.

3. *Consequences* (possible reinforcers)

(a) Mother shouts at him, scolds him or discusses with him what he has done

(b) She sends him out of the room

(c) Usually he gets his own way

Figure 6.5   An ABC analysis of disobedient behaviour.

Homework

Feedback.

Discipline

- What is discipline?

- Why is it important?

- How is it implemented?

See Appendix I.9 for the relevant handout.

Rules, roles and limits

- Why rules? Who rules?

- Setting limits.

- Where should they be drawn? Firm vs soft limits.

- Giving reasons for rules.

Giving instructions and commands

Looking back to the past; parents' experience of discipline/parenting.

Buzz session (break)

Physical punishment

- Advantages and disadvantages.
- The trouble with smacking.
- Roles: problems about authority and control.

See Appendix I.17 for the relevant handout.

Evaluation

Evaluation forms filled in and collected.

Homework

Record instances where you may have been tempted to smack your child, but used an alternative method. Describe how you felt before, during and after the episode.

▶ Session 8: Ignoring and time-out

Preliminaries

- Welcome and warm-up.
- Brief recap on main learning points from last week's session.
- Individual and group feedback on home task and overall progress.

Ignoring

- What is it and why use it?
- Parental examples are placed on the flip chart.
- Handout is provided.

See Appendix I.19 for the relevant handout.

Buzz session (break)

Time-out

- What is it and why use it?
- Parental examples of using time-out and variations.
- Ethical considerations.

See Appendix I.20 for the relevant handout.

Homework

Try out these techniques:

- Record the outcomes.
- Bring to the next session any difficulties.

Evaluation

- Provide evaluation forms and collect them.

▶ Session 9: Removing rewards and privileges

Preliminaries

- Welcome.
- Brief recap on main learning points from previous session.
- Reference made to the time-out procedure on the flip chart.
- Individual and group feedback on homework task. Also on how previous skills are being used together.

Removing rewards and privileges

- Explanation of removing rewards and privileges without confrontation.
- Parental examples.
- Role plays.

Buzz session (break)

Balancing positive and negative strategies

- Importance of keeping the emphasis on positive approaches where possible.
- Suggestive praise for this purpose.
- Balance sheet. What is your balance sheet of positive vs negative attention at this stage of the course?
- Role play of suggestive praise.

Problem-solving alternatives to punishment

- Brainstorm.
- Ideas on flip chart.

Homework

- Try out the methods discussed.
- Record the outcomes.

Evaluation

Evaluation forms filled in and collected.

▶ Session 10: Caring for yourself

This session deals with stress management.

Preliminaries

- Welcome.
- Brief résumé of main issues from previous session.
- Collect homework.

Homework

- Individual and group feedback.
- Discussion.

Parents' rights/children's rights

- Brainstorm a Parents' Charter by the group.
- Empowering – self-talk/self-help.
- Brainstorm a Child's Charter (compare the two charters).

Buzz session (break)

Stress management

- Fill in Figure 6.6, the Carer Stress Inventory.
- Relaxation exercises.

See Appendix I.12 and I.13 for the relevant handouts.

Evaluation

Evaluation forms filled in and collected.

Arrangements for a booster session

Name: _____

Date: _____

	YES	NO	CAN'T SAY
■ Do you feel your health is suffering?			
■ Do you get depressed by the situation?			
■ Do you sometimes feel that there is no end to your problems?			
■ Do you feel that you cannot cope any longer?			
■ Do you find it difficult to get a break from routine?			
■ Are you able to have visitors?			
■ Do you see your friends?			
■ Do you worry about accidents happening to...?			
■ Do you get angry and resentful with...?			
■ Do you feel embarrassed by...?			
■ Is your rest disturbed by...?			
■ Has your standard of living been reduced?			

Figure 6.6   Carer stress inventory.

▶ Session 11: Booster session

This session is a group reunion and offers an opportunity for troubleshooting.

Preliminaries

■ Welcome: update.

■ Individual and group feedback on overall progress.

■ Specific difficulties and any obstacles to change are discussed.

Evaluation results

Results from the evaluations are shared with individuals.

Booster session

- Reminders. Reassurance re. frequency of slippage ('behavioural drift').
- Main principles and ideas are reviewed, i.e. learning to be clear, using the ABC model, positive methods of encouraging 'desired' behaviour and setting limits.

Mutual support

If it is felt useful, parents exchange phone numbers and addresses in order that they can keep in contact (this may have been done before).

Conclusion

Group ends informally by parents going for a drink and/or meal.

CHAPTER SEVEN

The individual behaviour management course

This is the home-based version of the Child-Wise programme for individual parents to use with the practitioner.

▶ Objectives

When the experienced practitioner has studied the guidelines in the standard Child-Wise programme (Chapter Six) plus this administrative variation, and applied them in the parental home, he or she should be able to do the following:

1 Provide parents with strategies that have the potential to:

  (a) add to their confidence as carers;

  (b) increase their range of disciplinary methods;

  (c) introduce them to problem-solving skills;

  (d) reduce negative interactions with their offspring;

  (e) reduce their reliance on inappropriate means of punishment;

  (f) bring about improvements in the behaviour of the child,

2 Train parents in child management skills.

3 Teach them problem-solving skills.

The course is designed to help parents to gain, or regain, their self-confidence in managing the difficult behaviour of the children in their care. It is organised so as to create, restore or enhance mutually enjoyable parent–child interactions, and to reduce fraught, confrontational exchanges. The administration of the contents of the basic group version of the Child-Wise programme is meant to be flexible, the timing and order of core components designed to meet the needs of the individual parent and family.

▶ The Child-Wise home-based version

A home-based, individualised administration of the standard Child-Wise pro-gramme was piloted by a team of Portage workers, trained and supervised by a consultant clinical psychologist (Jenny Wookey, co-author of this book). Parents require (but often fail to receive) behavioural group leaders who receive regular supervision and support following rigorous training.

In the pilot studies, parents of young children were drawn (as clinical referrals) from a large catchment area which suffers from high unemployment, poor housing, high crime rates and other indices of serious dysfunction. While there is no intention to stereotype, denigrate, or patronise the many superb parents living on deprived estates, the fact is (as we have been told by mothers and seen for ourselves during home visits) that life in general is an uphill struggle, and parenting in particular is very difficult. Such problems increase exponentially when a disruptive child resides in the home.

The prevalence of serious disruptive behaviour is high in the children in these communities, and far exceeds the availability of therapeutic services. The risk factors for high attrition rates and low rates of success in behaviour management training (BMT) programmes in such environments are well known. Despite the significant, if sometimes restricted, advantages of group-based BMT programmes, more than one-third of families do not benefit from the group-based approach. There are parents who require something other than, or in addition to, the group-based method. They may find group settings somewhat daunting for a variety of reasons, for example:

- They may not be very articulate or they may lack self-confidence. They find the verbal methods of the group difficult to cope with.

- They do not share consensus values about life and child-rearing, and sense themselves to be 'outsiders'.

- Family life is disorganised, if not chaotic. To stick to regular appointments and do the homework tasks is too exacting.

- They are intensely private about what they see as their personal tragedies and 'failings' and cannot envisage public discussion of such issues, whatever the preliminary briefing and reassurance given.

- Child/spouse abuse in the family makes them wary of a public commitment to therapy, and possible disclosure.

- Parents may find the social interactions with other parents difficult to cope with.

- Not all clinical problems lend themselves to a group intervention.

- It requires the flexibility of content and therapeutic process of an individualised programme in order to adapt to the particular needs of some parents.

By no means all caregivers are motivated to change, or to care for their children. Initial individual casework may be necessary to bring them to the point of being ready to work behaviourally with their offspring.

Validation

The initial and subsequent tests of the home-based variation of the Child-Wise course were so successful that it now forms part of the regular service delivery in the Plymouth mental health area. The method (following training courses) has been adopted in other parts of the South-West region.

▶ Advantages of the home-based individual approach

The advantages that have emerged include:

- The capacity to tailor the programme to particular idiosyncratic elements of disruptive behaviour problems while addressing (following a functional analysis) some of the other difficulties that often accompany conduct disorders, e.g. feeding, and sleeping problems, enuresis, or truancy.

- The possibility of exploring in detail the content, meaning and sequences involved in behaviour change. More attention can be paid to the wider systemic influences that are unique to a particular family. Within the context of a group setting, members lose interest and concentration, sometimes becoming resentful if the focus stays too long on the specific concerns of one parent.

- Group work inevitably lessens somewhat the boundaries of confidentiality. Where the course is being conducted within a relatively close-knit community (such as areas targeted by the 'Sure Start' programme), confidentiality is vital.

- Visiting individual families at home is more likely to facilitate significant disclosure about the parent's child-rearing philosophy and personal history of being cared for and disciplined as a child. While intimate, personal information is often shared within groups, it is difficult for therapists to set safe limits of disclosure within and outside the group. Sensitive information may be disseminated that leads in some tense communities to malicious gossip or conflict between families.

- Regular meetings in the client's home are likely to encourage the development of a close collaborative working relationship between the therapist and the family. The tempo of the sessions is under better control of the therapist and parent. It is possible: (1) to pause (e.g. take 'time-out' of a whole session to discuss a domestic crisis that has arisen; (2) to repeat sessions so as to rehearse and master a difficult disciplinary strategy or review and refresh behavioural principles; and (3) to recover from an illness or take the child to the dentist.

- These diversions, if they are not to degenerate into defensive resistance, must be thoughtfully discussed and monitored, and certainly anticipated in contractual rules. The ultimate goal of the training – planned and negotiated change within a *sequence* of structured sessions that covers the core themes of the Child-Wise programme – must not be lost sight of in a series of informal, 'chatty' sessions.

- Some parents (particularly those with mental health problems, *moderate* learning difficulties, multi-level social stresses or limited verbal literacy skills) may need to have the programme modified in ways that meet their particular difficulties, but not at the expense of losing core skill-acquisitions. It is helpful: (1) to offer clear, simplified handouts; (2) to arrange for the client to work with a 'mentor' – a parent who has successfully completed the course; and (3) to reduce the use of the group-type 'Socratic' style of teaching in favour of more didactic, visual modes of training such as modelling, role play and video clips.

- Modelling of particular skills by the therapist, followed first by the parent's role play, and then immediate verbal or video feedback, are generally easier to initiate with shy individuals in the privacy of their homes.

- The practical arrangements (venue, timing of sessions, child minding, transport costs and unavailability) are not the drawbacks they prove to be in planning group meetings, or the obstacle preventing access to social and mental health services.

- This is truly a community intervention of the kind the Sure Start programme was funded to encourage. There is a parallel in the provision of general practice services. Children who are unwell are taken to a local GP and expect to return as and when needed. One visit is not expected to immunise the children for life. Parents do not train their offspring in one-off bursts of programmatic activity, never to return with reminders or renewed efforts when the child forgets the 'lessons' or refuses to abide by them. An individual, easily accessible psychological input that allows for repeats (booster sessions), for temporary setbacks, for changed circumstances (e.g. new problems of an older child) begins to approach the community-based 'attend when required' health model.

- Home visiting has the advantage of allowing the therapist to get a 'feeling' for the social context within which the disruptive behaviour occurs. The state of the home, availability of toys, attitude of the partner (if not engaged in the programme from choice), and the support of neighbours all provide valuable insights into the life-style of the parents and child.

- If the child is present, it is easier to assess reliably how effectively (if at all) the parenting strategies are being applied. This is in contrast to group work where parents are not (or seldom) followed up so as to observe how well the newly learned behavioural principles and techniques are translating to the home and other settings. Time-out is a good example of a method that parents describe reasonably well during the course, but tend to misapply at home when under pressure.

- Attrition rates are reduced significantly. It is difficult to 'opt out' of one's own home, which is not to say that the working contract neglects to describe how treatment can be mutually terminated.

Relationship and other 'therapeutic process' variables are essential in the tasks of encouraging optimistic expectations about the outcome of treatment, and creating positive attitudes about the trainers' approach to their problems. With these concerns in mind, Webster-Stratton and Herbert (1994) suggest a *collaborative* approach that aims to do the following:

- to build a supportive relationship with parents, often achieved by appropriate use of self-disclosure, humour and optimism, also by actively advocating for them (e.g. at the child's school) if appropriate;

- to empower parents, encouraging and validating their insights, helping them to change powerless thoughts, promoting self-empowerment (i.e. knowledge, skills and values), and building family and group supports;

- to teach by persuading, explaining, suggesting, adapting, giving assignments, reviewing;

- to 'translate', without being patronising, the cognitive, behavioural and developmental concepts into words that parents can understand and apply, and to enhance self-perceived efficacy (e.g. personal confidence).

▶ Reference

Webster-Stratton, C. and Herbert, M. (1994) *Troubled Families: Problem Children. Working with Parents: A Collaborative Process.* Chichester: Wiley.

CHAPTER NINE

The foster parents' behaviour management course

▶ Introduction

Rationale for the course

Foster carers provide a crucial service to some of the most vulnerable children who come to the attention of social services. These children have frequently had tragic histories; they may have very mixed feelings about being a 'looked-after' child, and some have no desire to be in the care of social services, and no wish to be separated from home and family, no matter the deprivation, neglect or maltreatment suffered there. Others have been taken into care for reasons of family misfortune and adversity, the traumatic loss of loving and caring relationships resulting in a deeply unhappy and insecure child.

These factors, as well as others, mean that looked-after children tend to be among the most challenging children to care for. The vast majority are cared for by foster carers. Whether in foster care or residential care, the very challenging behaviour that these children often present contributes to placements breaking down. Indeed, this is sometimes a factor in the reasons for parents seeking shared care of their children.

Aims of the course

This five continuous day (or weekly) course is designed to boost foster carers' confidence and skills in their efforts to manage such challenging behaviour. It seeks to do this:

- by developing carers' understanding of the problems often faced – and presented – by children looked after by social services departments;

- by enabling carers to identify and monitor the influences that trigger and maintain challenging behaviour;

- by teaching the carer to set reasonable/modest behavioural targets (goals);

- by developing their ability (e.g. behavioural methods) to reach these goals through effective behaviour management.

Format and philosophy of the course

The course follows a set agenda each day (or week) in order to ensure that a range of relevant issues is covered by the end of the course. However, the course is designed to be flexible and responsive to the needs of participants. The collaborative nature of the programme means that there is plenty of time for detailed discussion and sharing of ideas and expertise. Indeed, the collaborative nature of this programme is its hallmark. We hope to build as much of the programme as possible around the experiences and challenges of participants themselves, and to use these as the basis for sharing the knowledge and experience that the leaders have to contribute. The programme begins with two long sessions followed by three shorter ones, and the possibility of a further follow-up session is discussed at the end of session 5. All discussions in the group will be confidential to the group, except when information emerges relevant to child protection.

▶ Session 1: Introduction

Preliminaries

- Coffee/tea and welcome.
- Personal introductions.
- Rationale underpinning the training.
- Ground rules agreed.
- Future sessions discussed.

Sharing problems

- Participants describe the problems that concern them (written on flip chart).
- Foster parents' aims and expectations of the training.
- Video extract of an oppositional child or a brief case illustration.
- Disruptive behaviour defined.

Identifying target problems

Identifying, defining and noting down problems to work on as a project (see Figure 9.1).

Assessing challenging behaviour

Understanding the impact of a child's learning history by using the following techniques:

- Applied learning theory.
- The ABC of behaviour (brief exposition) (video example).

Trouble Spots Questionnaire

A: My foster child is disobedient *Circle one:* Often Seldom Never

B: It amounts to a real problem for me *Circle one:*

At home	Yes	No
Visiting	Yes	No
Shopping (or other public places)	Yes	No
At play-school or school	Yes	No
When out playing	Yes	No

C: My foster child gives me trouble:
Tick as appropriate

	Often	Seldom	Never
When getting ready (e.g. dressed) in the morning	❑	❑	❑
At mealtimes	❑	❑	❑
When going to bed	❑	❑	❑
Over staying in bed	❑	❑	❑
Over watching TV	❑	❑	❑
When asked to stop doing something	❑	❑	❑
Over keeping to the general rules	❑	❑	❑
Doing homework	❑	❑	❑
Running away (absconding)	❑	❑	❑

Figure 9.1 Identifying trouble spots. Alert yourself to the most likely 'trouble spots' in your life (when it comes to discipline) by filling in the questionnaire.

- The problem-solving approach.

- Describing in behavioural terms.

- Observation.

The social context of child care: attachments of children

- Attachment theory.

- Brief history of attachment theory (see Chapter two).

- Typology of attachments (e.g. secure/insecure attachments).

- Piecing together what you know from the foster child's past.

- Implications for psychopathology of childhood and adolescence.

- Help children develop skills to manage loss and attachments (brainstorm).

- The issue of trust – its crucial role in child-rearing.

- Discussion.

The fostering task

- Special dilemmas in 'looking after' (fostering) another person's child.

- The impact on the family/household.

- Understanding the impact of a child's learning history.

Foster children's needs

It is important to remember:

- that the child may now be experiencing new values, rules, routines, habits and trust;

- that it is all taking place in an environment (your home) that may not yet be familiar;

- that children generally remain touchingly loyal even to those who have not deserved it. It is important not to undermine their (probably vulnerable) dignity and self-esteem;

- that they may be bereaved following a loss or separation;

- that they may have lost trust in people, presenting a defensive, cynical and truculent persona;

- that they may not see why they are required to alter their behaviour;

- that change is usually painful and frequently resisted.

Foster parents' needs

- Foster parents identify their ideas on foster parents' needs and special difficulties (negatives and positives of fostering).

- Why parents/foster parents may find it difficult to attend to 'disturbed' or 'needy' children (dilemmas of their own children).

- Themes for discussion and reflection: (1) know your own family (your individual and family strengths); (2) know the foster children (his or her history of neglect, abuse, separations, etc.); their strengths and vulnerabilities.

- Discussion: questions and answers.

Are any of the following situations tiring 'disaster areas' for you?

- getting the child up in the morning;

- washing and getting him/her dressed;

- eating (breakfast and other meals);

- getting the child off to playgroup or school;

- getting the child to obey requests/instructions during the course of the day (e.g. 'Stop teasing your sister', 'Give your friend's toy back to him', 'Don't go out on the road');

- overcoming defiance of house rules (e.g. not washing hands after using the toilet, playing with fire, switching the TV channels endlessly);

- interrupting (by pestering) parents when they are in the toilet, on the telephone, cooking a meal, talking to someone, etc.;

- disrupting shopping trips by incessant 'I wants', putting items in the trolley, having tantrums, running away, etc.;

- quarrelling, fighting and refusing to share with brothers and/or sisters;

- not going to bed when asked; not staying there for the night.

▶ **2**   **For the record**

Answer these questions before and after completing the programme.

My child confronts me:

	Often	Seldom	Never
When getting dressed in the morning	☐	☐	☐
At mealtimes	☐	☐	☐
When going to bed	☐	☐	☐
Being made to stay in bed	☐	☐	☐
Over watching TV	☐	☐	☐
Getting him/her to wash/bathe	☐	☐	☐
When I'm busy on the phone or talking to someone	☐	☐	☐
When asked or told to do something	☐	☐	☐
When asked to stop doing something	☐	☐	☐
Over keeping to the house rules	☐	☐	☐
Doing homework in the car or on a bus	☐	☐	☐

Parents with disobedient youngsters tend to do the following: do you?

■ make too many commands;

■ use vague requests (e.g. 'Why can't you be good?' instead of 'Show me you can be good by not bullying your sister';

■ shout out their commands, out of sight, from a distance;

■ criticise too many trivial points in a child's conduct;

■ time requests/commands insensitively (without warning telling a child to go to bed in the middle of an exciting TV programme);

■ let a child get away with his/her 'misdemeanours';

■ make threats that remain unfulfilled;

■ use 'chain commands', i.e. issue a series of 'do this', 'do that', 'do the other' commands, or fire a barrage of negatives ('You mustn't!', 'You can't have', 'Stop it . . . or else');

■ convey 'messages' (wittingly or unwittingly) by tone of their voice, body language, or the constant criticism and attention paid to the child's 'bad points', that they dislike him or her;

■ make little quality time to share enjoyable moments (e.g. play with, or read to the child).

Answer the questions below, giving the settings in which you have difficult disciplinary problems with your child. Keep an ongoing record of progress during the course.

My child disobeys me:

	Often	Seldom	Never	It is a real problem for me
At home	☐	☐	☐	Yes/No
Visiting	☐	☐	☐	Yes/No
When shopping/other public places	☐	☐	☐	Yes/No
When out playing	☐	☐	☐	Yes/No
At playschool or school	☐	☐	☐	Yes/No

▶ **3**   **Making good behaviour worthwhile**

The 'rewards' that psychologists call 'positive reinforcers' (praise, encouragement, smiles and treats) influence behaviour. If you praise your child for behaviour you approve of, he or she will make the effort to earn more. Children are more likely to obey rules they dislike because they wish to have their parents' approval or avoid their disapproval. Such cooperation rests, in large part, on the foundation of a loving and respectful relationship between parent and child. Reward effort as well as success. Comment on how well they're doing when they try to do things that are difficult at first (like going alone to the toilet) or a nuisance (like tidying up) or awkward (like owning up when they have done something wrong). Your words of approval build up your youngster's self-confidence and self-esteem. Not all of his or her behaviours require external incentives; children also learn to solve problems simply for the joy of 'doing' or of achievement, which leads to self-reinforcement (self-statements such as: 'I am pleased with the way I coped with the exams'; 'Didn't I do well in the sports?').

Children do not behave well simply because parents expect them to. Behaviour has to be reinforced if the child is to learn. Some parents do not believe they should have to praise their children for everyday behaviours, while others do not know how or when to give praise and encouragement. Unless children are rewarded for keeping to the rules, they are likely to forget them or disobey them. Try noticing your child's good as well as bad behaviour. It is only too easy to take socially acceptable behaviour for granted by overlooking it.

Parents can be encouraged to respond positively to pro-social behaviours by praising them. If you want your child to be generous, acknowledge his or her actions when they share a favourite possession. Other examples of behaviours to praise might be:

- Greeting people in a friendly way.
- Good table manners.
- Going to bed at the first request.
- Playing quietly.
- Finishing homework.
- Feeding the pet animal.
- Taking the dog for a walk.
- Sharing a possession.
- Doing well at school.

There is a useful strategy that goes beyond the praise that follows the particular behaviour deserving of positive comment. It is called 'suggestive praise'. Here you use phrases to praise your child for *desisting* from previous transgressions (e.g. 'Thank you for getting ready for bed *without* a fuss'; 'I think you're a thoughtful girl *for not* getting into a temper because we couldn't go out').

This technique is useful when it is difficult (as many parents tell us) to find the sort of positive behaviour to praise. Similarly, children can be praised for effort, for 'neutral', or for quiet actions. At times it is necessary to try to observe many minor examples of behaviour which are pleasing. You might approach a child who (for example) is drawing happily (i.e. *not* being disruptive for a change) and say, 'You *are* drawing nicely, I feel really pleased'. Another example might be praising a child (who is usually aggressive when at play) when he hands a toy to another child, or allows that child to play undisturbed alongside him for a short time. Some parents comment that the technique seems somewhat contrived, and that they feel rather awkward at first. The method, however, if repeated, will gradually seem less artificial, and should pay dividends.

Yet another tactic is to 'create' or engineer a situation in which your child's cooperation (obviously a task of likely interest to him/her) will deserve your appreciation. If your child always seems to behave badly, you may have to model the behaviour you would like to see. Arrange for him/her to copy you doing something, and then praise the imitation. You might, for example, build a tower with your child, each taking turns to place a brick. When the tower is complete, share a little treat with him/her. Move on to encouraging your child to do the same with another child – this activity can be a 'starting point' for learning about cooperation, sharing and turn-taking.

Incentives

The best and simplest incentives are the social ones: noticing, showing enthusiasm, and a genuine interest, praising, smiling, hugging, clapping and, for young children, picking them up for a cuddle. Where there is a good relationship between the parents and child, he or she identifies with them and really wishes for their approval. When praising, there is no need for lengthy speeches! For example:

- 'I really enjoy it when you play calmly with your brother like this.'

- 'Thank you for doing what I said. I am really pleased when you do as I ask.'

- 'Good news! I'm really proud of your excellent school report.'

Be focused; don't flatter by exaggerating the praise.

It is not difficult to create a 'bad child self-image' if youngsters are monitored relentlessly for activities to denigrate. Build up your child's self-esteem by rationing the criticisms. Save them for actions that really merit concern. A crucial rule is not to mix praise and criticism, e.g. 'That's a good girl; kissing your little sister better. Never pinch her again or I'll show you what it feels like.' Such a double-edged message causes confusion and defeats the purpose.

Avoid 'negative injunctions' that are counter-productive. Clare, aged three, pulled her brother's hair. Her mother told her to say sorry. She screamed out: 'No, I won't!'. Her mother insisted. After a hesitation, Clare went to her brother and put her arms around him. Her mother said, 'I should think so! It's naughty. Don't do it again.' Clare's hand *immediately* shot out to pull his hair again. How should Clare's mother have handled this situation?

▶ 5   The when . . . then rule

The 'when . . . then' rule, sometimes referred to as 'Grandma's rule' or more technically as the Premack Principle, states: 'First you do what I want, then you do what you want.' You indicate your intentions, for example, by saying: '*When* you have tidied up, *then* you can go out to play.' When using a rewarding strategy, it is important to make it unambiguously clear to children that they will not be rewarded if they have previously *asked for* or *demanded* the reward (e.g. 'If I do my homework, then can I stay up late?'). That is the route to encouraging an 'I want . . . or else' attitude. The formula is 'when you . . . then I', *not* 'If I . . . will you?' With this policy, rewards are like 'contracts' and remain under your control. They are *not* 'bribes' the child manipulates to influence your actions.

Routines help children to operate on 'autopilot' when doing their daily tasks (eating, washing or going to bed) so that more can be achieved with little thought or effort. Habit is taught by repeating daily routines. Children feel secure if their day is regular and predictable. If going to bed always takes place from early in life with 'being tucked up' and a story-telling ritual, they usually depart for bed with little or no fuss. You pre-empt the exhausting bedtime battles so many parents have to suffer.

Giving very young children too much choice over when to go to bed or get up in the morning, what to wear, or what they eat for breakfast is a recipe for arguments, changes of mind, delays and tantrums. If you know what you do not want your son or daughter to wear, do not instruct them as follows: 'Get ready to go out. Go and put your clothes on.' This caution about being reasonably precise in your requests does not contradict the general proposition that children are individuals with rights, and should be given the opportunity to make choices and have a say on appropriate matters and at suitable times. What should be avoided are the cues (as potentially, in the example above) for lengthy 'Socratic' debates designed to delay, distract, or 'wind you up'. A potential minefield is the question instruction. For example, the instruction 'Will you please get dressed for mummy?' invites the answer 'No'.

The 'attention rule' states that a child will work for attention from others, especially parents. The attention can either be positive (for example, praise) or negative (for example, sarcasm, scolding, criticism) in nature. If the child is not receiving positive attention, he or she will work to receive negative attention. Remember the actress who said: 'I'd rather have bad publicity than no publicity at all.'

Some tips when giving praise:

- Praise immediately after the child has behaved well.

- Set consistent limits concerning which behaviours will receive praise (don't debase the currency by praising anything and everything).

- Praise with smiles, eye contact, and enthusiasm as well as with words.

- Praise when others are present.

- Some people give praise and then undermine it by being sarcastic or combining it with a punishing remark. This gives a 'mixed message' to a child and is one of the most counter-productive things a parent can do.

- Catch the child being good – praise small elements of behaviour, whether they are either good or simply non-disruptive (e.g. 'You are getting on well with your sister'). The latter is called 'suggestive praise'.

- Make sure your child knows exactly why he or she is being praised.

Older children are better able to understand delayed incentives. Symbolic rewards, such as stars or stickers on a chart, help to bridge the gap between action and a promised reward (say, a football match at the end of the week). Try your hand at designing sticker or colouring-in reward charts with your children.

One of the ironies you will find, if you try to analyse the ABC sequences of some of your confrontations with your child, is that they may be strengthening behaviours that you do not like.

Unacceptable + reinforcement = more unacceptable behaviour
behaviour (e.g. attention)

Unacceptable + no reinforcement = less unacceptable behaviour
behaviour

Experience is how we learn from our mistakes, but some parents do not allow their children to experience the consequences of their actions. They understandably wish to protect their child and/or ensure their 'happiness'. The natural consequences of a child's misbehaviour, if not forestalled or prevented, might be unpleasant (but important) reality checks. If parents always let him or her escape the consequences of their misdemeanours, the implications (outcomes) of the situation do not become apparent to them and they go on repeating the same misdeeds. In the long run they will end up with an unrealistic, immature (and in the worst-case scenario) delinquent child.

The 'natural/logical consequences' method

This method comes into play when parents decide *not* to intervene but let their children experience the natural (logical/reality) outcomes of their actions. A child must be old enough to understand what the natural consequences of his or her actions are likely to be. For the older child one warning of your intention to use the method is advisable. A good deal of thought is required here. To what extent (particularly with toddlers and teenagers) should you intervene (interfere?) to protect your child?

The consequences of a child's actions might be as follows:

■ The child won't get out of bed when his mother calls him in the morning, so he misses the school bus, is late for school and is punished by his teacher.

■ The teenager won't put her soiled clothing in the laundry basket as requested; they don't get washed. Eventually the day comes when the party clothes (the special ones) aren't there for her to wear.

It is important to remember that logical consequences are never to be used as a line of least resistance, or as an idle threat. You must be prepared to see through the likely consequences. Don't give in to tears and pleading. If you can allow your child or your teenager to experience these consequences (short of any which might cause them serious pain or hurt), he or she will learn from them without the necessity of nagging, grounding or fines.

If your child at mealtimes, for example, throws food on the floor, he or she is more likely to learn to behave if he or she has to do without the meal. If you always replace the food, he or she is likely to continue to be anti-social. Experience of reality provides the salutary lesson. So don't deny reality it's role, *unless* the implications or consequences of your child's behaviour are harmful, irreversible or, in some other way, dangerous or life-threatening.

Training children in self-control and relaxation techniques gives them control over actual or potentially stressful situations that lead to aggression or fearful panic. It is those situations which are beyond our control that people find most alarming. Suggesting something which the child can *say* to himself or herself in a crisis ('self-talk') can be surprisingly helpful: 'I am in control; I can manage. I am not going to be provoked.' Suggesting something which he or she can *do* – some *action* – adds to the child's sense of mastery.

The turtle technique is a simple self-control technique young children can be taught to use when they feel themselves becoming tense or angry. It is an imaginative combination of 'self-talk' (or 'self-instruction') and action (in the form of relaxation and problem-solving methods).

The turtle technique begins with a story to tell young children about Little Turtle. Little Turtle disliked school. In spite of his vows to stay out of trouble, he always managed to find it. For example, he would get angry and rip up all his papers in class. One day when he was feeling especially bad, he met a tortoise. The old tortoise addressed him: 'Hey, there, I'll tell you a secret. Don't you realise you are carrying the answer to your problem around with you?' Little Turtle didn't know what he was talking about. 'Your shell – your shell!' the tortoise exclaimed. 'That's why you have a shell. You can hide in your shell whenever you get that feeling inside you that tells you are angry. When you are in your shell, you can have a moment to rest and figure out what to do about it. So next time you get angry, just go into your shell.'

The next day when Little Turtle started to get upset at school, he remembered what the tortoise had advised, so he closed his eyes, pulled in his arms close to his body, put his head down so his chin rested against his chest (going into his shell), and rested for a while until he knew what to do. He told himself to stay calm, count up to 10, work out quietly what to do next. The story ends with the teacher coming over and praising him for his reaction. Little Turtle receives a very good report card that term.

The story is thus used to teach a child to respond like the wise old tortoise when the prompt word 'turtle' is given.

The following exercises are suggested for coping with stress and tension. The exercises all involve the following general steps:

- Lightly tense a given group of muscles (as listed below) and hold this tension for a slow count of five while holding your breath.

- During the above step, focus your attention on the sensations in the part of your body that has been brought under tension.

- At the end of five seconds, breathe out, relax the tense muscles *as much as possible*, focusing your mind on the new relaxed sensations in that part of your body.

- While letting go (as above), think of the words 'calm yourself' and 'relax'.

- Allow your muscles to relax completely and, in your mind, compare the feelings of tension just experienced with the relaxation you now feel.

The particular exercises are as follows:

- *Arms:* Clench the fists and tighten the muscles of both arms, holding your arms still and straight out in front of you.

- *Legs:* From a lying position, raise both legs (or one, if preferred) about 12–18 inches from their resting position, point the toes and stiffen the legs so that thigh and calf muscles are brought under tension. Repeat with the other leg if necessary.

- *General torso:* Pull the shoulders back, bringing shoulder blades together, push the chest forward and out and, at the same time, use appropriate muscles to *pull in* the stomach, making a hollow in that part of your body.

Remember, each of the above exercises is immediately preceded by taking a deep breath, creating tension, and holding it for five seconds, then exhaling while letting go the tension and saying the word 'relax' to yourself. In each case, try to focus your mind on the part of your body that has in turn been made tense and relaxed.

Don't try to hurry the programme of exercises, which should take about 20 minutes or so. After each separate exercise, allow a minute or so for fuller relaxation to take place and for you to concentrate on the pleasant sensations that relaxation brings.

A common problem that arises with siblings when a child is on a behavioural programme is often voiced as follows: 'I am good and get nothing; Janice is naughty and gets stickers and other rewards.' The reasons for the token economy could be explained to her sibling (e.g. 'Your mum and dad need to help Janice to be better behaved. She finds it difficult to learn because, as you've complained, she is so fidgety and overactive'). It would be better still to have a reward system they can all contribute to as a family, perhaps one that leads by collectively earned stickers (recorded on charts) to family treats such as family outings.

A popular system with young children is to make a 'shop' with a shoebox, decorating it with the help of the child. Work out, with your child, a list of inexpensive items the child can earn with tokens (counters) or accumulated points (recorded in a notebook). In another list set out the tasks or 'good' behaviours you wish to encourage. It is always worth discussing these goals with older children, seeking their opinion and justifying (rejecting if you cannot) items they feel are unreasonable or impossible. Work out a tariff of what successful performance is worth, in tokens or points. The harder the task, the higher the amount earned. Ensure that:

- early efforts are manageable so as to motivate the child;

- the interval between success and reward is not too lengthy;

- the system is fully understood;

- the system is seen to be fair.

The child goes shopping for items at their different prices at the end of the day or morning/afternoon. Rewards should be reviewed and varied (e.g. a 'menu' of different items and treats) to maintain their incentive value.

A notebook or 'ledger' for older children records points for good behaviour/tasks in the credit column. The withdrawal of points for misdemeanours or tasks refused would be registered in the debit column. The penalty of withdrawal must not be arbitrary: the 'costs' of bad behaviour in the loss of points must be clearly understood by the child. Older children could earn privileges rather than tangible rewards.

Many children receive pocket money on a weekly basis. This can have sums deducted (although not according to most foster home regulations) as 'fines' for unacceptable behaviour. As with all punishments, it requires thoughtful planning. A total deduction on Monday would leave no room for reductions from Tuesday to Sunday, and thus no incentive for the child to desist from continuing the unwanted behaviour. For young children, a jar with marbles representing (say) the 25 10ps they get weekly, with an additional money bonus while doing the programme, is used. Behaviour that is prohibited (e.g. swearing, hitting, clinging and whining) is fined at a marble at a time for each misdemeanour.

A blameless week means a full jar, and full pocket money plus the bonus. The marbles may, of course, be withdrawn until they are few in number or the jar emptied, the result being little or no pocket money.

Another variation could be the addition of marbles for cooperation (specifically defined behaviour), e.g. for helping small brother with his homework, or helping mother and father to do the shopping.

You should *phase out* the use of artificial reinforcers (stickers, stars, tokens or points) when the child has learned a skill well, or when persistent problematic behaviour has been rectified. Ease out these so-called symbolic rewards on a gradual basis – giving occasional rewards (e.g. more tasks for the same rewards; more verbal reinforcements). Tell the child of your intentions. Make use of plentiful social reinforcers and the occasional treat by way of acknowledging your child's continuing efforts.

Your child may 'work hard' (e.g. escalate the dramatic effects of the outburst) to regain the previous reinforcement where you gave in to stop the frightening tantrums, and thus may get 'worse' before getting 'better'. You will need to steel yourself for this initial increase in the behaviour you want to eliminate; but don't lose heart as the method usually works if you consistently stick to your guns. In the case of tantrums, if they are essentially attention-seeking rather than manipulative, it is important to ask yourself whether your child is getting sufficient attention (e.g. quality time with you) or notice, when behaving well.

Time-out has been shown to be an effective penalty. The child is taken away from the setting where unacceptable behaviour is being reinforced. In practice, it is best to choose from two acceptable forms of time-out:

1 *Activity time-out* where the child is simply barred from joining in an enjoyable activity but still allowed to observe it, for example, having misbehaved, he or she is made to sit out of a game.

2 *Room time-out* where he or she is socially isolated at the far end of the room on a naughty chair or in the hallway (not somewhere that is either enjoyable/frightening).

Time-out may last from three to five minutes. In practice, 'activity' or 'room' time-out is preferred to 'seclusion' time-out, a method parents often use by sending the child to their room for an unspecified period of time. (Should a child's bedroom be a place of punishment? On the other hand, its possible contents of computer games and television may make it a haven of pleasure – a contra-indication for this method.)

The following points should be borne in mind:

- Time-out is unlikely to succeed unless it is part of a *dual* strategy in which you supplement the method with positive reinforcement for alternative, more acceptable ways of behaving.

- The more 'costly' your child finds it to be removed from the limelight or from whatever he or she finds rewarding about misbehaving, the more effective is time-out likely to be. (This is why time-out should be as boring as possible – it then becomes a real penalty.)

- Don't make a fuss when the child comes out of time-out.

- Time-out, if administered firmly, insistently but gently, usually results in the child's going to the 'naughty' chair at the end of the room relatively peacefully. But it does provoke rebellious, aggressive behaviour in a minority of children.

You are the best judge of when this approach is counter-productive. With older, physically strong, resistive children, time-out may simply not be feasible. You may then need to consider response-cost.

Notes

- Don't threaten time-out unless you are prepared to carry it through.

- Give three to five minutes in time-out (no more!), with repeats if the child continues to behave badly. (It may be helpful to give the children an egg-timer to hold.)

- Ignore the child while he or she is in time-out.

- Be prepared for him or her to test your resolve, persistence and consistency.

- Limit the number of behaviours for which time-out is used.

- Check that the child is getting his or her fair share of quality time/positive attention.

- Where the child is very young and/or distressed in time-out it is best to wait for a *pause* in the crying or (say) tantrum and then bring the child out, before the time-out would normally end. It is important not to reinforce the misdemeanour by making the ending of time-out coincide with its continuation. The pause is the critical moment for action.

▶ **21**   **Out shopping**

Your child knows, or thinks, he or she has you at a disadvantage by his or her knowing use of cunning tactics when you are vulnerable in public places, whether in supermarkets, on public transport, at the park, during a church service or a visit to the doctor. His or her highly visible (indeed, audible) demands, tantrums and disobedience are acutely humiliating and anger-arousing. In such situations you might try the methods an Australian psychologist, Michael Griffin, suggests to cover these situations:

- Prepare your child for each visit by explaining how you want him or her to behave. If you are shopping, stop outside the shop and go over the rules and consequences.

- Indicate precisely which behaviours are unacceptable. Where possible, give him or her some task to carry out during the outing, for example, helping to find the items on a shopping list. If possible, help your child to practise the correct behaviours while still at home.

- Carry a 'black book' on outings, and record in it unacceptable behaviours by writing a short description in front of your child (such as 'wandered off in supermarket'). Warn your child first that you will record the behaviour in the black book if it doesn't stop immediately. Also *praise your child for acceptable behaviour* and record this in the book on a separate page (such as 'helped carry shopping'). When you return home, you can convert the good and bad behaviours noted in the book into tokens or points won or lost. The 'costs' may lead to the loss of, say, television-watching time.

- Quite often, rewards and penalties can be applied on the spot. For example, you could reward a child for staying with you in the supermarket by buying a small treat as you leave. State the condition before you begin shopping: 'You can have a comic if you stay close by me while I am shopping.' Penalties can also sometimes be applied on the spot, for example, by removing your child to your car for five minutes, while you remain outside it (don't leave your child in a car!). If travelling in a car, you might stop for a few minutes as a penalty, refusing to speak to the child until he or she behaves.

As a first step in achieving or restoring a happier relationship, we encourage parents to play with their children for at least 10 minutes every day, offering them some pointers on ways to play successfully with their children. A happy playtime between parents and children not only fosters warm relationships, but also helps children develop the vocabulary they need for communicating their thoughts and feelings. It also helps them learn the social skills of turn-taking and to understand the feelings and perspectives of others, and to develop their non-verbal/performance skills.

These are the major points we highlight:

- Let your child lead and direct the play session.

- Give the child time to think and explore.

- Avoid competition (e.g. by building a bigger/better . . . painting a prettier . . .).

- Avoid criticism of your child's efforts and ideas.

- Watch and describe his or her play.

- Resist the temptation to give too much assistance.

- Don't keep on asking questions or making 'educational alterations'.

- Be prepared to take part in imaginative scenarios.

- Children enjoy directing role plays and making up fantasy games.

- Give simple praise at times, e.g. 'What a lovely house', 'That's a fast car'.

- Limit the number of toys for a play session and provide a selection to suit your child's age and developmental level.

- Attend to calm play; change the activity if he or she gets over-excited.

- Avoid 'rough-and-tumble' and other over-arousing play near bedtime.

- Choose toys which provide flexible, varied and imaginative opportunities.

- Avoid frustrating (e.g. over-complicated, incomplete, fragile, broken) toys.

Knowledge is power and one aim of our course is to empower parents by giving them the means to problem-solve children's difficult behaviour for themselves. Making sense of persistent and therefore worrying behaviour from your child can often be achieved by using the 'ABC of behaviour' formula. Here is the basic method:

> **A**ntecedent events are those events that precede, lead up to, and set the stage for (say) disobedient behaviour.
> **B**ehaviour (the disobedient actions), which in turn leads to certain
> **C**onsequences – positive or negative – for the child and parent(s).

If you think about and watch the settings of your child's behaviour, it may be that he or she behaves in a non-compliant way, or has a tantrum on some occasions but not others; that is, some situations seem to act as cues to behave in a particular way.

The A term

The A term – antecedents – indicates *eliciting* or *discriminative* stimuli (as they are known technically) that trigger unacceptable behaviour, or indicate that such actions will result in a pleasant outcome (reward). The C term – consequences of an action – may point to 'pay-offs' that maintain the unwanted behaviour.

Children tend to tailor their behaviour to the particular places in which, and different persons with whom, they find themselves. Children tend to look around them, consider the rules, the adult's determination, how other children behave and what is expected of them, then they adapt their behaviour accordingly. It is instructive to observe a parent who is used – perhaps even resigned – to being disobeyed. That parent is likely to be 'going wrong' on one or more of the following (on the 'A' side of the ABC formula) when making a request:

■ standing well away from the child;

■ using a tentative, pleading tone of voice;

■ asking a question ('Will you put your toys away for mummy?');

■ showing a resigned expression, eyes glazed with the expectation of defeat; accepting defeat passively;

■ doing the job herself (e.g. putting away the toys);

■ timing it insensitively;

■ asking the child to do something inappropriate for his/her age (e.g. expecting a semi-literate pupil not to feel inadequate in lessons about literature).

In some cases, especially with disabled children, it is most effective to change the antecedents to unacceptable behaviour. It may require an alteration in the setting in which a hyperactive child studies, making the workplace less stimulating and distracting; it may be the boring lessons that need attention as they put the pupils to sleep or instigate more interesting mischief; it might necessitate less time gossiping with friends at the supermarket when there is already a reluctant 3-year-old in tow.

The C term

If Jo does something, and as a result of her action something pleasant happens to her, then she is more likely to do the same thing in similar circumstances in the future. When psychologists refer to this pleasant outcome as the *positive reinforcement* of behaviour, they have in mind several kinds of reinforcers:

- *tangible rewards*, such as sweets, treats, pocket money;

- *social rewards*, such as attention, a smile, a pat on the back, a word of encouragement;

- *self-reinforcers*, such as the ones that come from within and which are non-tangible: self-praise, self-approval, a sense of pleasure or achievement;

- *activities*, such as pictures to colour in (in stages), cutting out pictures and stickers, watching TV, listening to music, playing board games, puzzles, visits, helping mother/father;

- *privileges*, such as staying up late, choice of meal, extra pocket money, extra-long story from parent, outing with parent (football match, cinema).

Does the following description ring any bells for you?

> Gary is 6 years old and his mother often says, 'He's so different from his older
> brother. If I'd had him first I would never have had another child!' Although Gary
> can sit still to watch television for short periods, he is otherwise restless and easily
> distracted, constantly moving about from one place to another and from one thing
> to another. He talks loudly, gets excited easily in groups. He never finishes anything,
> and is difficult to put to bed at night. His parents feel exhausted from the constant
> need to monitor his unsafe behaviour, and they report that disciplinary methods
> don't seem to work.

Gary was diagnosed at the Child Development Centre as suffering from Attention
Deficit Hyperactivity Disorder (AD/HD for short).

Few family doctors, paediatricians, child psychiatrists or clinical child psychologists will not have been faced, in recent times, by a parent waving an article
from a magazine, or book, or citing a TV programme, about the 'problem flavour'
of the decade: Attention Deficit Hyperactivity Disorder and the 'magical cure',
Ritalin. Many bemused healthcare professionals, hazy about the nature of, and
the appropriate choice of treatment (are these children really ill?) or inexpert in
the prescription of Ritalin (and concerned about side-effects and ethical issues)
have wilted before the pressure of understandably harassed parents (and teachers)
of extremely difficult-to-manage disruptive children.

Advocates for social and familial models of AD/HD believe it is dangerous
to invent medical conditions to explain social difficulties and suggest that many
children who would previously have been called 'badly behaved' are now being
labelled 'medically ill'. They suggest that it is important to investigate behaviour
patterns, home life and upbringing for the answers to questions about the causes
of AD/HD. Certainly, to date, no single biological defect has been identified
which can adequately explain the symptoms of AD/HD.

It has certainly been the hope of many professionals and, not least, parents
that the identification of an underlying biological cause would go some way to
redress the balance of 'perceived blame' for families, removing the shame when
some professionals and members of the public point the finger at parents' alleged
inadequacies.

What do we know about AD/HD?

A child may (1) have poor attention but not be markedly overactive; (2) he or
she may be overactive but able to concentrate quite well; but (3) most AD/HD
children have *both* problems. What stands out in the 'shell-shocked' mind of
any mother or father of such a child is of someone who is a sheer 'mobile
disaster area'. With his or her short attention span, rapidly changing goals and
insatiable touching and demanding, combined with a rather 'muscular' ham-
fisted approach to the world, they leave in their wake broken toys, smashed

Copyright © 2004 John Wiley & Sons, Ltd.

ornaments and upset grocery shelves – if the mother is brave enough to take them to a supermarket.

The apparently incessant motion of the seriously overactive child gives the impression that he or she is driven by a motor, and, to continue the metaphor, by a motor which is tuned to turn over too quickly, even when it is idling. Where they do differ from other children who are also often naughty and exuberant is in the extent of their unwillingness or inability to inhibit their anti-social and frenetic activities in the home or classroom.

Their inability to brook *any* thwarting or delay in the gratification of their 'wants' is indicative of a more general problem of low frustration tolerance – a sign of immaturity. The hyperactive child has an uncanny gift for choosing to do things which compel parents to intervene either to prevent injury to him- or herself (they are impulsive and fearless) or to others. Their attention-seeking succeeds to a degree that is so all-embracing that parents feel themselves to be on a 24-hour per day duty rota.

What causes AD/HD?

The majority of studies of hyperactivity have failed to establish a *single, specific* medical cause. What one can say is that the hyperactive child is a child with some kind of physical (constitutional) problem, but frequently with the added complication of difficult-to-manage, poorly controlled behaviour. While little is yet certain, researchers believe that a fault (most likely inherited) in the neurological system causes poor self-control and hyperactivity. A fashionable and plausible view is that deficits (inherited) in the ability to attend may be biochemical in origin.

There is growing speculation that neurotransmitters play an important role in the AD/HD symptomatology. The catacholamine hypotheses suggest that an under-availability of dopamine and norepinephrine in the brain is a major determinant, although precise mechanisms which reduce availability have not been delineated. As one researcher put it: 'Inconsistent results seem to be the one predictable phenomenon regarding research into causes of AD/HD.'

Whatever the causes of AD/HD, the central feature, poor concentration, makes learning – at home and at school – extremely difficult for some hyperactive children. The repercussions are devastating! It is especially a problem in boys – four boys are diagnosed as AD/HD for every girl. The activity problems may improve somewhat as the child matures toward adolescence, but the poor, anti-social conduct tends to persist if not treated, and, indeed, may get worse.

Who can diagnose?

Children with attention deficits and/or hyperactivity benefit from an evaluation by a multidisciplinary team. The team might be based in a medical, educational, mental health, paediatric or other agency. Effective professional collaboration is essential in order to identify all the child's needs.

Treatment

Although medication (particularly the stimulant Ritalin) does facilitate the *short-term* (i.e. day-to-day) management of hyperactive children in about 75 per cent of cases, it is not a panacea; it has little or no impact on the social, academic or psychological adjustment of these youngsters in the long run. Primary effects are the improvement of attention span with the reduction of disruptive, inappropriate and impulsive behaviour. Compliance with authority figures' requests and commands is increased. This provides a 'window of opportunity' for behavioural work with the child and his or her family, often carried out in conjunction with medication. Medication alone has not been demonstrated to continue its positive results after its cessation. On its own it is not a long-term solution to AD/HD.

If your doctor recommends medication, Dr Russell Barkley (1995, p. 250), one of the foremost experts on AD/HD, recommends you put the following questions (which I have paraphrased) to him or her:

1 What are the effects, and side-effects, of this medication for the short term and the longer term?

2 What doses will be used, and by what schedule (time intervals) should they be given?

3 How often would you see my child to review his or her progress while on the medication?

4 When should the medication be halted temporarily to see if it is still required for his or her AD/HD?

5 Are there foods, beverages or substances to be avoided while my child is on his or her prescribed medication?

6 Will you be in contact with the school to determine how he or she is responding to the treatment in that setting? Or am I expected to do that?

7 What should I do if my child accidently takes an overdose?

8 Do you have a fact sheet about the medication that I can read?

Behaviour therapy for AD/HD

A behavioural approach to treatment (of the kind described in this course) may render the use of drugs unnecessary, or (in combination with medication) make less likely any prolonged drug dependence or the abdication of personal parental responsibility.

A favourable outcome for AD/HD children can be expected if parents and teachers (or other carers) provide understanding, supportive and positive discipline. Children with AD/HD need extra supervision, especially confident and consistent parenting, and good liaison with the school. The results of firm, *positive* parenting and good cooperation and assistance from the health and educational services can be most encouraging. Negative, endless criticism and put-downs by parents and teachers to these undoubtedly challenging, indeed, exhausting children are likely to lead to further problems: low self-esteem, poor relationships and schoolwork, and possibly serious anti-social behaviour.

Many children with AD/HD grow up to be highly successful members of society. However, neglect of their particular inborn difficulties of coping with life can lead to a stormy adolescence and emotionally/behaviourally disturbed adulthood.

▶ Reference

Barkley, R. (1995) *Taking Charge of ADHD: The Complete Authoritative Guide for Parents.* New York: Guilford Press.

The case of Freddie B, aged 8 years, illustrates some of the points made in this manual, in particular the successful use of cognitive and self-control training. Here was a child who was disrupting his home by bouts of aggressive behaviour. This was a crisis intervention, because there was a distinct possibility of his being taken into care. His parents could not cope with him because (they claimed) he was out of control at times. The assessment was made on the basis of visits (accompanied by a trainee on placement) to Freddie's home, a school visit to his school (for the blind), some 30 miles from his home village, and outings with him to a swimming pool.

Initial contact and background

Freddie presented an intensely aggressive 'picture' on the first two visits. If we had made an assessment in generalised global terms based on this session, it would have been highly misleading. The trainee, making an orientation visit, met Freddie on his return from school. He swore at her and then attacked her physically. The author (MH) paid the second visit with the trainees and was met by obscenities. These died away when Freddie was taken by us for a drive in the car. Indeed, after his truculent and physically and verbally violent beginning, Freddie came over as an intelligent, friendly and articulate boy. Despite his near-complete blindness, he could get around (e.g. in the swimming pool) with remarkable ease and agility. He was robust, vigorous and powerful. We gradually developed a mutually warm and friendly relationship. Freddie tended (probably out of loyalty to his parents) to be reserved about some of his worries at home and at school, but, in almost imperceptible stages, he confided about these.

He lived in a terraced house with his middle-aged mother (a woman with a serious heart condition) and his retired father. Although he had no siblings, a girl of his age, Alice, who lived a few doors away, was very much like a sister to him and seemed as much at home in his house as he was.

Some of the refinements of a leisurely assessment had to be curtailed as the case was an emergency one. The parents were at their wits' end, and were arguing about whether or not to have Freddie at the weekends because of his difficult behaviour and its adverse effect on Mrs B's deteriorating health. The parents were threatening to 'walk out' in relation to each other and in relation to Freddie. Social Services were involved in the case.

Assessment

An ABC assessment of Freddie's difficult behaviour suggested that it was highly specific to a refusal to return in the school bus to his school for the blind, on a Sunday afternoon. His behaviour leading up to, and particularly at, the point of being asked to go to the bus waiting outside his home consisted of what the parents called 'spasms'. These involved an escalation from grumbling,

naughty behaviour. By attending to positive actions parents make them more likely to occur. Explain simply and clearly what is expected of them.

Guideline 10: Promoting independence

Giving young people responsibility gives them the opportunity to become independent and confident.

Guideline 11: Be empathic

Encourage parents to listen carefully to what their child says. When children are expected to be seen and not heard, their parents suppress undesirable behaviour without paying attention to the unspoken underlying needs and messages. Children's communications are often in code. As professionals or as parents we need to be empathic, and listen with the 'third ear' to what they are saying.

For parents and professional people who work with children, it is vital to be able to communicate understanding. A dialogue with a young child requires respect and skill. Messages should preserve the child's and parents' self-respect; statements of understanding should precede statements of advice or instruction. The child who comes home saying, 'I hate school' learns that it is not everything about school that she dislikes when her mother says, 'It's been a bad day today, hasn't it; you have maths which you don't feel confident about on Monday – are you still feeling a bit anxious about it?'

Course evaluation forms

▶ **Evaluation of your course**

Name:
Session No.:
Date:

Session ratings

Please take a minute to think about today's session. Keeping your impressions of the session in mind, try to match the descriptions in each item on the following pages with what you thought and felt. Circle the numbers of the statements which best describe your experience. (Ask someone if you have questions.)

1. **I realised something new about myself as a parent:** As a result of the session, I have now understood something new about myself as a parent. I see why I did or felt something.

1	2	3	4	5
not at all	slightly	somewhat	quite a lot	very much so

2. **I realised something new about children:** As a result of the session, I have now understood something new about my child or children in general.

1	2	3	4	5
not at all	slightly	somewhat	quite a lot	very much so

3. **The course is clarifying problems for me to work on:** As a result of this session, I now have a clearer sense of how I need to change in relating to or managing my child; in other words, what my goals are.

1	2	3	4	5
not at all	slightly	somewhat	quite a lot	very much so

4. **I have made progress towards knowing what to do about problems:** As a result of this session, I have worked out possible ways of coping with a particular situation or problem.

1	2	3	4	5
not at all	slightly	somewhat	quite a lot	very much so

5. **I feel the course leaders understand me:** As a result of this session, I now feel more understood – that someone else really understands what is going on with me or what I'm like as a parent with a difficult child.

1	2	3	4	5
not at all	slightly	somewhat	quite a lot	very much so

6. I feel closer to my child: As a result of the course (the sessions up to now), I have come to feel that I understand my child's behaviour better; this has made me feel closer to him/her.

1	2	3	4	5
not at all	slightly	somewhat	quite a lot	very much so

7. I feel my parenting and child management skills have changed for the better: There is an improvement in my skills as a parent as a result of what I have learned in all these sessions up to now.

1	2	3	4	5
not at all	slightly	somewhat	quite a lot	very much so

8. I feel more in control of events; I am more confident as a parent.

1	2	3	4	5
not at all	slightly	somewhat	quite a lot	very much so

9. Put a cross on that part of the line which describes whether your child's behaviour is:

_____

much worse	somewhat worse	just the same	somewhat better	much better

▶ Child-Wise parenting skills course evaluation form

Name . . . .   Session No. . . . .   Date . . . .

Please rate this week's session by circling a number for each question which best represents how you feel.

Key: 0   1   2   3   4
         Very poor   Poor   Fair   Good   Very good

1. How well was the session organised?	0	1	2	3	4
2. How well was the programme material presented?	0	1	2	3	4
3. Were the topics covered in sufficient depth?	0	1	2	3	4
4. How were the practical issues explained?	0	1	2	3	4
5. How well did you feel supported by the leader(s)?	0	1	2	3	4
6. How well did you feel supported by others in the group?	0	1	2	3	4
7. How well do you feel your opinion/contribution was valued?	0	1	2	3	4
8. To what extent do you feel you are making progress at this stage of the course?	0	1	2	3	4

Further questions:
Which aspects of the session did you find most useful?

Are you having difficulties with the homework tasks?   YES/NO
If yes, what are the problems?

Child-Wise selection interview

<u>CONFIDENTIAL</u>

1. *GENERAL*
   Name of Child . . . .
   Date of Birth . . . .
   Address . . . .
   . . . .
   School . . . .
   Telephone . . . .

   Name(s) of Parent(s) (Age(s)) . . . .
   Marital or Cohabiting Status . . . .
   Address if separated (M/F) . . . .

   Telephone . . . .

2. *CLINICAL*

   (a) Parent(s)' statement of problem(s): (Supplement Eyberg/Rutter Scales)
   see references

   (b) Onset/development of problem(s):

(c) Prioritising of problems(s) (i.e. desire for change)

1. . . . .
. . . .

2. . . . .
. . . .

3. . . . .
. . . .

(d) Child's comments/views

3. SOURCE OF THE REFERRAL

Referral from: . . . .
. . . .

Other agencies involved: . . . .
. . . .
. . . .

Help previously given by: . . . .
. . . .
. . . .

Any special circumstances: (e.g. Child Protection Register): . . . .
. . . .

4. CHILD'S HEALTH

Health problems

(a) Are there any things which he/she is not allowed to do because of his/her health? *Like playing games or swimming?*
Please answer YES or NO

Yes ☐   No ☐

If YES, what are they?

. . . .
. . . .
. . . .

(b) Has he/she seen your family doctor recently?

Yes ☐   No ☐

If YES, please give the reason(s) for seeing the doctor.

. . . .
. . . .
. . . .

(c) Has he/she been to a hospital Casualty or Out-patient Department?

Yes ☐ No ☐

If YES, how many times has he/she been to the hospital?

☐

(number of times)

If YES, please give the reason(s) for attending the hospital.

. . . .
. . . .
. . . .

(if check-up, please give reason for check-up):

. . . .
. . . .

If YES, please give the name of the hospital:

. . . .

(d) Has he/she been admitted to hospital (that is, to stay in hospital overnight)?

Yes ☐ No ☐

If YES, how many times has he/she been admitted to hospital?

☐

(number of times)

If YES, what was the reason for being in hospital?

. . . .
. . . .

If YES, what was the name of the hospital?

. . . .

(e) Speech
   Is child's speech: (tick one)
   Entirely normal? ☐
   Speech not quite distinct or clear but easily understandable? ☐
   Understandable with some difficulty? ☐
   Understandable with considerable difficulty? ☐
   Hardly understandable at all? ☐

(f) Fits
   Has he/she had a fit at any time in his/her life

(that is, a spell, convulsion or any other attack that a doctor has called a fit)?

Yes ☐   No ☐

If YES, when was his/her last fit?

. . . .

If YES, describe them.

. . . .

. . . .

(g) Weakness or paralysis
Has he/she got any weakness or paralysis of his/her arms or legs?

Yes ☐   No   ☐

If YES, please describe it.

. . . .

. . . .

(h) Medicines
Has he/she had to take any medicine or tablets regularly for longer than 2 weeks?

Yes ☐   No   ☐

If YES, what was it for?

. . . .

(i) Does he/she need any special diet or are there any foods he/she is not allowed to eat?

Yes ☐   No   ☐

If YES, say what it is (they are).

. . . .

. . . .

If YES, who advised the diet or said he/she should not eat certain foods?

. . . .

(j) Does he/she need any extra care that you've not already mentioned *(for example, taking to toilet, getting up at night, wheelchair, etc.)?*

Yes ☐   No   ☐

. . . .

. . . .

(k) **Energy**
   Has your child a normal amount of energy?   (tick one)
   Bounding with energy   ☐
   Just normal amount of energy   ☐
   Tired, sluggish or lacking in energy   ☐
   Very sluggish, tired or lacking in energy   ☐

(l) **Hearing**
   Has your child any difficulty with hearing?
   Yes, marked difficulty ☐   **Yes, slight difficulty** ☐   **No** ☐
   If YES, describe:

   . . . .
   . . . .

(m) **Has your child difficulty with sight even when wearing glasses?**
   Yes, marked difficulty   ☐
   Yes, slight difficulty   ☐
   No   ☐
   If YES, describe:

   . . . .
   . . . .

(n) **Coordination**
   Is your child clumsy or poorly coordinated for his/her age?
   Yes, marked clumsiness   ☐
   Yes, slight clumsiness   ☐
   No   ☐
   If YES, describe:

   . . . .
   . . . .

5. DEVELOPMENTAL HISTORY

(a) **Was the pregnancy normal? (e.g. physical/stress)**

   Yes   ☐   **No**   ☐

   If No, give details.

   . . . .
   . . . .

(b) **Was the birth normal? (e.g. delivery: full term/Caesarian/duration of labour)**

Yes ☐ **No** ☐

If No, give details.

. . . .

. . . .

(c) **Birth weight** . . . .

(d) **Early complications?** (e.g. difficulty in sucking/convulsions/jaundice)

. . . .

(e) **Early temperament** (tick one)

Easy ☐

Slow to warm up ☐

Difficult ☐

Details: . . . .

. . . .

At what age did the child: (tick one box in each section)

(f) **Sit without support on a flat surface** *(such as the floor or on a bed if supported by any cushions, etc.)?*

8 months or earlier	☐
9–10 months	☐
11–12 months	☐
13 months or later	☐
Not known	☐

(g) **Walk without help or holding on?**

17 months or earlier	☐
18–21 months	☐
22–24 months	☐
25 months or later	☐
Not known	☐

(h) **First use single words with meaning** *(excluding 'mum', 'dad', 'hello', or 'bye bye')?*

18 months or earlier	☐
19–24 months	☐
25–30 months	☐
31 months or later	☐
Not known	☐

(i) First put three words together?

    24 months or earlier □
    25–30 months □
    31–36 months □
    37 months □
    Not known □

(j) Gain consistent bowel control
(exclude 'accidents' occurring less often than once per month)?

    30 months or earlier □
    31–36 months □
    37–42 months □
    43 months or later □
    Not yet gained control □
    Not known □

(k) Gain consistent bladder control during the day
(exclude 'accidents' occurring less often than once per month)?

    30 months or earlier □
    31–42 months □
    43–54 months □
    55 months or later □
    Not yet gained control □
    Not known □

6. SOCIAL HISTORY

Family Tree (Genogram) (on a separate sheet of paper)
(if the child is present get him or her to help with it, if possible)

(a) Parental situation
    Child living with 2 natural parents □
    Child living with birth mother alone (i.e. not with father) □
    Child living with birth mother and father substitute □
    Child living with birth father alone (i.e. not with mother) □
    Child living with birth father and mother substitute □
    Child living with third person (not either parent) □
    Child living in an institution of any kind □
    Not known □

(b) Reason for anomalous parental situation
    Not applicable (i.e. rated 0 on 'parental situation') □
    Parents separated or divorced □
    Parents or parent dead □
    Not known □
    Other: specify . . . .
    . . . .

(c) Is the child in the care of the local authority, or in a children's home or in a foster home—or has he/she ever been so?

No	☐
Yes, currently	☐
Not now, but has been in the past	☐
Not known	☐

If Yes, specify . . . .

. . . .

(d) Have either parent or any of the other children been delayed in their development or 'behind' in their schooling?

No	☐
Yes	☐
Not known	☐

If Yes, specify . . . .

. . . .

(e) Have either parent of any of the other children had great difficulty in learning to read?

No	☐
Yes	☐
Not known	☐

If Yes, specify . . . .

. . . .

(f) Marital/cohabiting partner relationship

. . . .

7. PARENTS' HEALTH
(please ring the correct answer)

■ Do you feel tired most of the time?	Yes	No
■ Do you often feel miserable or depressed?	Yes	No
■ Do you often get worried about things?	Yes	No
■ Do you usually have great difficulty falling asleep and lie awake at night?	Yes	No
■ Do you worry a lot about your health?	Yes	No
■ Do you often get extremely angry?	Yes	No
■ Do you often get fearful for no obvious reason?	Yes	No
■ Are you easily upset or irritated?	Yes	No
■ Are you afraid of meeting people?	Yes	No
■ Do you often feel jittery?	Yes	No

- Is your appetite poor?   Yes   No
- Do unimportant things get on your nerves?   Yes   No
- Does your heart often race frighteningly?   Yes   No
- Have you ever had a nervous breakdown?   Yes   No

Questionnaire completed by Mr/Mrs/Ms . . . .

8. EARLY PARENT–CHILD INTERACTIONS/RELATIONSHIPS

Parent's confidence . . . .
Parent's enjoyment of baby/toddler . . . .
Baby's crying pattern . . . .
Baby's sleeping pattern . . . .
Baby's eating pattern . . . .

9. LIFE EVENTS (CHILD AND FAMILY)

Separations . . . .
Trauma (e.g. bereavements/accidents) . . . .
. . . .

10. SIBLINGS

Details (names/ages) . . . .
Relationship with referred child . . . .
Problems: 1.   . . . .
             2.   . . . .
             3.   . . . .
             4.   . . . .

11. SCHOOLING

Name of school: . . . .
Teacher: . . . .
Progress at school: . . . .

Absence from school   Frequent   ☐   Infrequent   ☐
Reports of disruptive behaviour   Yes   ☐   No   ☐
If Yes, give details . . . .
. . . .
Other problems at school . . . .
. . . .

12. COGNITIVE FUNCTIONING

IQ (where available) . . . .
Specific learning difficulties   Yes   ☐   No   ☐
If Yes, give details . . . .
. . . .

13. *SUPPORT NETWORK*

Can you confide in/obtain support from:

	Yes	No
Partner	☐	☐
Parent(s)	☐	☐
Children	☐	☐
Friends/neighbour	☐	☐
G.P.	☐	☐

Comments: . . . .
. . . .

14. *TYPICAL DAY IN THE LIFE OF:*

Main areas/times of confrontation: . . . .
. . . .

(use a separate piece of paper)

15. *BALANCE SHEET*

Child's 'good' points   Child's 'bad' points

16. *FUNCTIONAL (ABC) ANALYSIS OF MAIN BEHAVIOUR PROBLEM(S)*

(see assessment procedures)

Background to the Child-Wise course

The original programme was developed in the 1970s at the Centre for Behavioural Work with Families and published under the title *Behavioural Treatment of Children with Problems* (London: Academic Press, 1987) by one of the present authors (MH). The course evolved over several years with the help of post-graduate social work and clinical psychology trainees and doctoral research students at Leicester University. The method was adapted for workshops with teachers, held regularly under the auspices of the Leicestershire Education Department, at Baumanor Hall. Versions for health visitors and social workers were designed and tested.

Following a move to manage the NHS Child Psychology services in Plymouth, I was joined by Jenny Wookey, a consultant clinical psychologist, in evaluating the service delivery of the Child-Wise programme at the Plymouth Child Development Centre. With the help of colleagues we further broadened and tested the repertoire of applications. In association with Professor Geraldine McDonald from Bristol University we randomised a controlled research study of training foster parents using the manual. Sixty foster mothers and fathers from all over the South-West of England achieved ratings on 'knowledge of behavioural methods' and on 'self-confidence in behaviour management' of the children in their care – results that were significantly higher than those of the foster parents in the waiting list control group. The brochure for this course is given as an example for you to use in your course.

In a 1994 manual, *Troubled Families: Problem Children*, Carolyn Webster-Stratton and MH highlighted their collaborative style of working with groups of parents with conduct-disordered children. Based at Washington University in the USA, Carolyn Webster-Stratton is well known for her creative use of video and puppetry as teaching materials.

A (1999) TV film *The Trouble with Kids* was made in Bristol for HTV and Channel 4 television – a real-life, real-time portrait of parents of disruptive children attending the course over a period of several weeks. We occasionally use clips from these films to illustrate behavioural methods. But it is a good idea to collect one's own video material from the widely available stock of commercial and TV channel programmes.

▶ **Validation studies**

The Child-Wise parenting skills course, based as it is on a collaborative model of working, has been successful to an encouraging extent in changing parental behaviours, feelings and attitudes and those of their children. Sources for this programme (*inter alia*) are:

*Brassington, S. (1996) Reducing the risk of physical, emotional abuse and neglect in families. D Clin Psych thesis, University of Exeter.
*Gill, A. (1997) What makes 'parent training' groups effective? Promoting positive parenting through collaboration. PhD thesis, University of Leicester.
Herbert, M. (1995) A collaborative model of training for parents of children with descriptive behaviour disorders. *British Journal of Clinical Psychology*, 34, 325–342.
Herbert, M. and Iwaniec, D. (1981) Behavioural psychotherapy in natural home-settings. *Behavioural Psychotherapy*, 9, 55–76.
*John, F. (1996) An investigation into the process of outcome of a parent training group. D Clin Psych thesis, University of Exeter.
Neville, D., King, L. and Beak, D. (1995) *Promoting Positive Parenting*. Guildford: Arena.
*Payne, Jan (1996) Evaluation of a parent training course, D Clin Psych dissertation, University of Plymouth.
Scott, M.J. and Stradling, S.G. (1987) The evaluation of a group parent training programme. *Behavioural Psychotherapy*, 15, 224–239.
*Sutton, C. (1988) Behavioural parent training: a comparison of strategies for teaching parents to manage their difficult young children. PhD thesis, University of Leicester.
Sutton, C. (1995) Parent training by telephone: a partial replication. *Behavioral and Cognitive Psychology*, 21, 11–24.
Webster-Stratton, C. and Herbert, M. (1994) *Troubled Families: Problem Children*. Chichester: Wiley.
Webster-Stratton, C. and Herbert, M. (1995) What really happens in parent training? *Behavior Modification*, 17, 407–456.
*Wilson, Sarah (1995) Evaluation of a parent training course, MSc dissertation, University of Exeter.

*These researchers conducted evaluative studies of programmes along somewhat similar lines to the authors' programme. These were Doctoral/MSc studies supervised by M. Herbert. Andy Gill's extensive study has demonstrated (*inter alia*) significant improvement in problematic children's behaviour and increases in parental skill and confidence. He runs a Fun and Families programme on the Internet. Carole Sutton validated telephone-based treatment.

Sarah Wilson, in a 1996 Master's qualitative study of treatment outcomes and attributions of parents who had attended Child-Wise courses, reported that they generally experienced the collaborative style of working as (*inter alia*) 'user-friendly', engaging and confidence-boosting.

Table A.I below indicates the evaluation by a sample of 50 parents who attended Child-Wise programmes, their attitudes to aspects of the course and changes it brought about. This study was conducted for us by Jan Payne from the University of Plymouth.

Table A.1   Parent skills group survey

Questions	Yes (%)	No (%)
1. Able to attend without crèche?	52	48
2. Helpful talking about child's behaviour?	100	0
3. Partnership with Martin and Jenny?	84	16
4. Helpful hearing about others' children?	96	0*
5. Useful to have a friend or relative attend?	64	36
6. Helpful sharing own ideas about parenting?	100	0
7. Passed on ideas from group to others?	80	20
8. Helpful hearing about others' childhood experiences?	76	24
9. Benefit from refresher sessions?	88	12
10. Helpful talking about own childhood?	64	36
11. Helpful listening to others' ideas about parenting?	84	16
12. More confident as a parent?	83	17
13. Relationship with child less enjoyable?	0	100
14. More in control as a parent?	80	20
15. Parenting skills increase?	88	12
16. Relationship with child more enjoyable?	76	24
17. Less confident as a parent?	0	100
18. View child with more understanding?	92	8
19. Less in control as a parent?	0	100
20. Child easier to manage?	72	28

Note: *One respondent failed to answer.

▶ **Brochure**

Information about the Child-Wise parenting skills course

What brings fathers and mothers together every week for two hours of serious discussion and debate, a lot of fun and laughter, and at the end of each session, 'homework' tasks to carry out during the following week? Some of the parents would say it was originally a growing sense of helplessness – a loss of confidence in their parenting skills; others would describe their despair at having to give in so often to a wilful, ever-demanding child. One or two might admit to fear and guilt: the fear of losing their self-control, guilt at the feelings of dislike for a child they should (and usually do) love.

Children are usually a source of great pleasure and wonder to their parents. These joys are sometimes tempered by the concern and heavy sense of responsibility that also accompany parenthood; the pleasure may be transformed into anxiety and the wonder into puzzlement when the child begins to behave in a peculiar or erratic manner. The youngster who has not, at some stage of his or her development, been the cause of quite serious worry to their carers must be unique. The discovery of this fact in a group of similarly hard-pressed parents comes as a welcome and hugely reassuring insight. Parents are not taught how to bring up children so it is not surprising that they occasionally have trouble in raising their offspring.

Some children, for a variety of reasons, social, physical, psychological or a combination of influences, display challenging behaviour of a more extreme kind. A child may have a difficult temperament and is more resistant to discipline than other children, or because stresses on the family make it particularly hard to keep up the difficult work of parenting. Our job is to work with you and to consult with you so that the relationship between you and your child is more positive and so that you can achieve your goals. The way our programme works is to meet each week with a group of parents (with similar children) in order to study and discuss together parent–child interactions and child behaviour management. We work together as a team. This means that as we decide together on some disciplinary strategies for you to try out at home with your child, you become the experts on what works or doesn't work with your child. When things don't work, you bring this information back to us and we put our heads together to come up with a more effective strategy for the problem. You see, we all have a contribution: what we can offer is alternatives, information and support, and what you can offer is your own ideas and consistency in implementing the best methods for your situation.

If you wish for more information, please contact us.

Department of Social Policy and Social Work
University of Oxford
Barnett House
32 Wellington Square
Oxford OX1 2ER
England

SOCIAL SCIENCE LIBRARY

Manor Road Building
Manor Road
Oxford OX1 3UQ
Tel: (2)71093 (enquiries and renewals)
http://www.ssl.ox.ac.uk

This is a NORMAL LOAN item.

We will email you a reminder before this item is due.

Please see http://www.ssl.ox.ac.uk/lending.html
for details on:

- loan policies; these are also displayed on the notice boards and in our library guide.

- how to check when your books are due back.

- how to renew your books, including information on the maximum number of renewals.
  Items may be renewed if not reserved by another reader. Items must be renewed before the library closes on the due date.

- level of fines; fines are charged on overdue books.

Please note that this item may be recalled during Term.